THE MERRY WIVES OF WINDSOR

THE MERRY WIVES OF WINDSOR

William Shakespeare

The paper in this book is produced from pure wood pulp, without the use of chlorine or any other substance harmful to the environment. The energy used in its production consists almost entirely of hydroelectricity and heat generated from waste materials, thereby conserving fossil fuels and contributing little to the greenhouse effect.

This edition published 1995 by
Wordsworth Editions Limited
Cumberland House, Crib Street, Ware,
Hertfordshire SG12 9ET

ISBN 1 85326 267 6

Printed and bound in Denmark by Nørhaven
Typeset in the UK by R & B Creative Services Ltd

INTRODUCTION

The Merry Wives of Windsor is the only citizen comedy that Shakespeare wrote, though this was a popular genre with his contemporaries such as Jonson and Dekker. Tied to an occasion, the play was apparently commissioned by Queen Elizabeth, probably in 1598 or 1599, to celebrate the Garter Feast of St. George's day when the installation of knights who were inducted into the Garter Order took place at Windsor.

The Merry Wives of Windsor is also unique in that it is the only one of Shakespeare's comedies to be set specifically in England. Comedy traditionally examines social relations, and here Shakespeare displays a whole network of these. Windsor is a microcosm where the power of middle-class tradespeople such as Page and Ford stems from acquired wealth rather than ancestry. Their wives aspire to sophistication and are attracted to Falstaff because of his association with the court, yet their pleasures are essentially rustic and their morality is straightforward. The Pages and Fords duly have their colourful entourage of assorted individuals, and naturally draw other groups to them. The inter-action of these social groups, each with their different accents and manners, provides the central conflict of the play and makes for a dazzling richness of language.

The Welsh parson, Sir Hugh Evans, is employed as tutor to the Pages's children and his singular manner of speech coupled with eccentricity is hilarious in performance. Evans and the French medical doctor, Caius, thought by Mistress Page to be a fine catch for her daughter Anne because of his court connections, are duped by the host of the Garter Inn, and their efforts to avenge themselves become a hectic sub-plot. The play's main action concerns the Pages's efforts to find a husband for their daughter, and Falstaff and Fenton's efforts to relieve their impoverished circumstances. Another group to arrive on the scene from Gloucestershire comprises Justice Shallow, his nephew Slender (another suitor to Anne Page) and their servant Peter Simple. With gullibility implicit in the names, they represent the landed gentry and provide another effective comic contrast of both class and accent.

Many critics cannot endure what is seen as the diminishment of one of Shakespeare's greatest creations, namely Falstaff. Following his rejection by Prince Hal, Falstaff is now discredited and in debt. Far from manipulating people and circumstances as he was wont to do, others now 'consult together against this greasy knight' (II, 1). Removed from his proper milieu, Falstaff has become the mere scapegoat of a comic intrigue. His manifold humiliations are certainly demeaning, but whereas Falstaff is fundamentally destroyed at the end of the History plays, here the comic convention itself ensures his survival. Both he and Fenton gain from their surprising encounter with the citizens of Windsor, whom they had expected to find easy prey. They are forced to reassess their views, and whereas Fenton learns what love is, Falstaff reaches a depth of self-knowledge that director Terry Hands finds 'totally seductive'. Equally, the Windsor citizens gain from the experience too. Ford has to acknowledge his wife's virtue and hence the folly of his jealousy, and the Pages have to overcome their instinctively puritanical suspicion that Fenton 'is of too high a region' and 'knows too much' (III. 2).

Conflicting evidence within the text makes it difficult to determine a seasonal setting for *The Merry Wives of Windsor*, and scholarly opinion is divided between spring and autumn. The play is mostly in prose and its comedy has all the trappings of farce, but frequent allusions to the proximity of Windsor Castle and to the rituals of the Order of the Garter raise the comic tone by invoking a more significant social structure than that presented by the Windsor citizens, with their comfortable routines of possets and fireside gossip and Cotswold sports. The slapstick of the Herne the Hunter interlude lacks any pretensions to formality, but the very device of the masque carries underlying implications of a ceremonial action, just as he does in the play scenes in other comedies such as *Love's Labour's Lost* and *A Midsummer Night's Dream*, here too Shakespeare dabbles with illusion and reality. With a plot that is heavily reliant on comic deceit, *The Merry Wives of Windsor* repeatedly affirms the power of illusion.

Dismissed by many critics as a mere professional farce that was knocked-off in a couple of weeks to satisfy a royal command, the play was nevertheless tremendously popular with Queen Elizabeth I, who was a devotee of Falstaff and had long yearned to see him in love. Its rollicking action has continued to delight audiences ever since, and Terry Hands dismisses the theory of its swift execution on the grounds of the play's rich language. He finds The Merry Wives of Windsor 'Shakespeare's warmest and richest comedy'.

Details of Shakespeare's early life are scanty. He was the son of a prosperous merchant of Stratford-upon-Avon, and tradition has it that he was born on 23rd April 1564; records show that he was baptised three days later. It is likely that he attended the local grammar school, but he had no university education. Of his early career there is no record, though John Aubrey states that he was, for a time, a country schoolmaster. How he became involved with the stage is equally uncertain, but he was sufficiently established as a playwright by 1592 to be criticised in print. He was a leading member of the Lord Chamberlain's Company, which became the King's Men on accession of James I in 1603. Shakespeare married Anne Hathaway in 1582, by whom he had two daughters and a son, Hamnet, who died in childhood. Towards the end of his life he loosened his ties with London, and retired to New Place, his substantial property in Stratford that he had bought in 1597. He died on 23rd April 1616 aged 52, and is buried in Holy Trinity Church, Stratford.

Further reading:

Shakespeare and the Idea of the Play by Anne Righter, 1962

Citizen Comedy in the Age of Shakespeare by Alexander Leggatt, Toronto 1973

Introduction to The Merry Wives of Windsor by Terry hands, the Folio Society, London 1950-1976

Shakespeare II, (Writers and Critics series) by Gareth Lloyd Evans, Edinburgh 1969

The scene: Windsor

CHARACTERS IN THE PLAY

SIR JOHN FALSTAFF
FENTON, *a young gentleman*
ROBERT SHALLOW, *a country justice*
ABRAHAM SLENDER, *his wise cousin*
FRANK FORD, GEORGE PAGE — *two citizens of Windsor*
WILLIAM PAGE, *a boy, son to Master Page*
SIR HUGH EVANS, *a Welsh parson*
DOCTOR CAIUS, *a French physician*
The Host of the Garter Inn
BARDOLPH, PISTOL, NYM — *irregular humorists, followers of Falstaff*
ROBIN, *page to Falstaff*
SIMPLE, *servant to Slender*
JOHN RUGBY, *servant to Doctor Caius*
JOHN, ROBERT — *servants to Master Ford*
MISTRESS FORD, MISTRESS PAGE — *the merry wives*
ANNE PAGE, *her daughter, beloved of Fenton*
MISTRESS QUICKLY, *servant to Doctor Caius*

THE MERRY WIVES OF WINDSOR

[I. I.] *A street in Windsor, before the house of Master Page*
Trees and a seat

Justice SHALLOW, SLENDER, *and Sir* HUGH EVANS *approach, holding lively conversation*

Shallow [*hotly*]. Sir Hugh, persuade me not: I will make a Star-chamber matter of it. If he were twenty Sir John Falstaffs, he shall not abuse Robert Shallow, esquire.

Slender [*nodding*]. In the county of Gloucester, justice of peace and 'Coram.'

Shallow. Ay, cousin Slender, and 'Custalorum.'

Slender. Ay, and 'Ratolorum' too; and a gentleman born, master parson, who writes himself 'Armigero,' in any bill, warrant, quittance, or obligation—'Armigero.'

Shallow. Ay, that I do, and have done any time these 10 three hundred years.

Slender. All his successors—gone before him—hath done't: and all his ancestors—that come after him—may... They may give the dozen white luces in their coat.

Shallow [*proudly*]. It is an old coat.

Evans. The dozen white louses do become an old coat well: it agrees well, passant: it is a familiar beast to man, and signifies love.

Shallow [*coldly*]. The luce is the fresh fish—the salt fish is an old †cod. 20

Slender. I may quarter, coz.

Shallow. You may—by marrying.

Evans. It is marring indeed, if he quarter it.

Shallow. Not a whit.

Evans. Yes, py'r-lady; if he has a quarter of your coat,

there is but three skirts for yourself, in my simple conjectures; but that is all one...If Sir John Falstaff have committed disparagements unto you, I am of the Church, and will be glad to do my benevolence, to make atone-
30 ments and compromises between you.

Shallow. The Council shall hear it! it is a riot.

Evans. It is not meet the council hear a riot: there is no fear of Got in a riot: the council, look you, shall desire to hear the fear of Got, and not to hear a riot: take your vizaments in that.

Shallow. Ha...o' my life, if I were young again, the sword should end it.

Evans. It is petter that friends is the swort, and end it: and there is also another device in my prain, which perad-
40 venture prings goot discretions with it....There is Anne Page, which is daughter to Master Thomas Page, which is pretty virginity.

Slender. Mistress Anne Page? She has brown hair, and speaks small like a woman.

Evans. It is that fery person for all the 'orld, as just as you will desire, and seven hundred pounds of moneys, and gold, and silver, is her grandsire, upon his death's-bed—Got deliver to a joyful resurrections!—give, when she is able to overtake seventeen years old....It were a goot
50 motion if we leave our pribbles and prabbles, and desire a marriage between Master Abraham and Mistress Anne Page.

†*Shallow.* Did her grandsire leave her seven hundred pound?

Evans. Ay, and her father is make her a petter penny.

†*Shallow.* I know the young gentlewoman. She has good gifts.

Evans. Seven hundred pounds, and possibilities, is goot gifts.

Shallow. Well, let us see honest Master Page...Is Falstaff 60
there?

Evans. Shall I tell you a lie? I do despise a liar as I do despise one that is false, or as I despise one that is not true: the knight, Sir John, is there, and I beseech you be ruled by your well-willers: I will peat the door for Master Page....[*knocks and calls*] What, ho! Got-pless your house here!

Page [*from within*]. Who's there?

Evans. Here is Got's plessing, and your friend, and Justice Shallow, and here young Master Slender...that 70
peradventures shall tell you another tale, if matters grow to your likings.

Page [*opens the door and comes out*]. I am glad to see your worships well...I thank you for my venison, Master Shallow.

Shallow. Master Page, I am glad to see you: much good do it your good heart: I wished your venison better—it was ill killed...How doth good Mistress Page?—and I thank you always with my heart, la! with my heart.

Page. Sir, I thank you. 80

Shallow. Sir, I thank you: by yea and no, I do.

Page. I am glad to see you, good Master Slender.

Slender. How does your fallow greyhound, sir? I heard say he was outrun on Cotsall.

Page. It could not be judged, sir.

Slender. You'll not confess...you'll not confess.

Shallow. That he will not. 'Tis your fault, 'tis your fault: 'tis a good dog.

Page. A cur, sir.

Shallow. Sir: he's a good dog, and a fair dog—can there be 90
more said? he is 'good and fair'....Is Sir John Falstaff here?

Page. Sir, he is within: and I would I could do a good office between you.

Evans. It is spoke as a Christians ought to speak.
Shallow. He hath wronged me, Master Page.
Page. Sir, he doth in some sort confess it.
Shallow. If it be confessed, it is not redressed; is not that so, Master Page? He hath wronged me, indeed he hath, at a word he hath: believe me—Robert Shallow, esquire,
100 saith he is wronged.
Page. Here comes Sir John.

Sir JOHN FALSTAFF, BARDOLPH, NYM, and PISTOL come from the house

Falstaff. Now, Master Shallow, you'll complain of me to the king?
Shallow. Knight, you have beaten my men, killed my deer, and broke open my lodge.
Falstaff. But not kissed your keeper's daughter!
Shallow. Tut, a pin! this shall be answered.
Falstaff. I will answer it straight. I have done all this... That is now answered.
110 *Shallow.* The Council shall know this.
Falstaff. 'Twere better for you, if it were known in counsel: you'll be laughed at.
Evans. Pauca verba; Sir John—goot worts.
Falstaff. Good worts! good cabbage...Slender, I broke your head: what matter have you against me?
Slender. Marry, sir, I have matter in my head against you, and against your cony-catching rascals, Bardolph, Nym, and Pistol. [They carried me to the tavern, and made me drunk, and afterward picked my pocket.]
120 *Bardolph.* You Banbury cheese! [*he draws his sword*
Slender. Ay, it is no matter.
Pistol. How now, Mephostophilus! [*he also draws*
Slender [*faintly*]. Ay, it is no matter.

Nym [*pricks him with his sword*]. Slice, I say; pauca, pauca: slice! that's my humour.

Slender [*desperate*]. Where's Simple, my man? can you tell, cousin?

Evans [*comes between them*]. Peace, I pray you...[*the three withdraw*] Now let us understand...[*takes out a note-book*] There is three umpires in this matter, as I under- 130 stand; [*writes*] that is, Master Page (fidelicet Master Page) and there is myself (fidelicet myself) and the three party is (lastly and finally) mine host of the Garter.

Page. We three, to hear it and end it between them.

Evans. Fery goot. I will make a prief of it in my note-book, and we will afterwards 'ork upon the cause, with as great discreetly as we can. [*he writes again*

Falstaff. Pistol.

Pistol. He hears with ears.

Evans [*looks up*]. The tevil and his tam! what phrase is 140 this, 'He hears with ear'? why, it is affectations.

Falstaff. Pistol, did you pick Master Slender's purse?

Slender. Ay, by these gloves, did he—or I would I might never come in mine own great chamber again else—of seven groats in mill-sixpences, and two Edward shovel-boards, that cost me two shilling and two pence a-piece of Yed Miller...by these gloves!

Falstaff. Is this true, Pistol?

Evans. No, it is false, if it is a pick-purse.

Pistol. Ha, thou mountain-foreigner! Sir John, and
master mine, 150
I combat challenge of this latten bilbo:
Word of denial in thy labras here;
Word of denial; froth and scum, thou liest!

Slender. By these gloves, then 'twas he.
[*pointing at Nym*

Nym. Be avised, sir, and pass good humours: I will say

'marry trap' with you, if you run the nuthook's humour on me—that is the very note of it.

Slender. By this hat, then he in the red face had it: for though I cannot remember what I did when you made
160 me drunk, yet I am not altogether an ass.

Falstaff. What say you, Scarlet and John?

Bardolph. Why, sir, for my part, I say the gentleman had drunk himself out of his five sentences.

Evans. It is his five senses: fie, what the ignorance is!

Bardolph. And being †fap, sir, was, as they say, cashiered ...and so conclusions passed the careers.

Slender. Ay, you spake in Latin then too: but 'tis no matter; I'll ne'er be drunk whilst I live again, but in honest, civil, godly company, for this trick: if I be drunk,
170 I'll be drunk with those that have the fear of God, and not with drunken knaves.

Evans. So Got-'udge me, that is a virtuous mind.

Falstaff. You hear all these matters denied, gentlemen; you hear it.

During this talk ANNE PAGE, *bearing wine, comes from the house, with Mistress* PAGE *and Mistress* FORD

Page. Nay daughter, carry the wine in—we'll drink within. [*she obeys*

Slender. O heaven...this is Mistress Anne Page!

Page. How now, Mistress Ford!

Falstaff. Mistress Ford, by my troth, you are very well
180 met: by your leave, good mistress. ['*kisses her*'

Page. Wife, bid these gentlemen welcome...Come, we have a hot venison pasty to dinner; come, gentlemen, I hope we shall drink down all unkindness.

[*all but Slender enter the house*

Slender. I had rather than forty shillings I had my Book of Songs and Sonnets here...

SIMPLE comes up the street

How now Simple, where have you been? I must wait on myself, must I? You have not the Book of Riddles about you, have you?

Simple. Book of Riddles? why, did you not lend it to Alice Shortcake upon Allhallowmas last, a fortnight afore Michaelmas? 190

SHALLOW and EVANS return to look for SLENDER

Shallow. Come coz, come coz, we stay for you...[*taking him by the arm*] A word with you, coz...marry, this, coz... there is as 'twere a tender, a kind of tender, made afar off by Sir Hugh here...Do you understand me?

Slender. Ay, sir, you shall find me reasonable; if it be so, I shall do that that is reason.

Shallow. Nay, but understand me.

Slender. So I do, sir.

Evans [*at his other side*]. Give ear to his motions; Master Slender, I will description the matter to you, if you be capacity of it. 200

Slender. Nay, I will do as my cousin Shallow says: I pray you pardon me—he's a justice of peace in his country, simple though I stand here.

Evans. But that is not the question: the question is concerning your marriage.

Shallow. Ay, there's the point, sir.

Evans. Marry, is it: the very point of it—to Mistress Anne Page. 210

Slender. Why, if it be so...I will marry her upon any reasonable demands.

Evans. But can you affection the 'oman? Let us command to know that of your mouth, or of your lips: for divers philosophers hold that the lips is parcel of the mouth: therefore, precisely, can you carry your good will to the maid?

Shallow. Cousin Abraham Slender, can you love her?

Slender. I hope, sir, I will do as it shall become one that
220 would do reason.

Evans. Nay, Got's lords and his ladies! you must speak possitable, if you can carry-her your desires towards her.

Shallow. That you must...Will you—upon good dowry—marry her?

Slender. I will do a greater thing than that, upon your request, cousin, in any reason.

Shallow. Nay, conceive me, conceive me, sweet coz: what I do is to pleasure you, coz: can you love the maid?

Slender. I will marry her, sir, at your request; but if
230 there be no great love in the beginning, yet heaven may decrease it upon better acquaintance, when we are married and have more occasion to know one another: I hope upon familiarity will grow more contempt: but if you say, 'marry her,' I will marry her—that I am freely dissolved, and dissolutely.

Evans. It is a fery discretion-answer; save the fall is in the 'ort 'dissolutely': the 'ort is, according to our meaning, 'resolutely': his meaning is goot.

Shallow. Ay...I think my cousin meant well.

240 *Slender.* Ay, or else I would I might be hanged, la!

ANNE PAGE returns

Shallow. Here comes fair Mistress Anne; [*he bows*] Would I were young for your sake, Mistress Anne!

Anne [*curtsies*]. The dinner is on the table. My father desires your worships' company.

Shallow. I will wait on him, fair Mistress Anne.

Evans [*hurries in*]. Od's plessed-will...I will not be absence at the grace. [*Shallow follows*

Anne [*to Slender*]. Will't please your worship to come in, sir?

Slender [*simpering*]. No—I thank you forsooth—heartily; 250
I am very well.

Anne. The dinner attends you, sir.

Slender. I am not a-hungry, I thank you, forsooth...[*to Simple*] Go, sirrah, for all you are my man, go wait upon my cousin Shallow...[*Simple goes in*] A justice of peace sometime may be beholding to his friend, for a man; I keep but three men and a boy yet, till my mother be dead: but what though? yet I live like a poor gentleman born.

Anne. I may not go in without your worship: they will 260
not sit till you come.

Slender. I'faith, I'll eat nothing: I thank you as much as though I did.

Anne [*impatient*]. I pray you sir walk in.

Slender. I had rather walk here—I thank you. I bruised my shin th'other day with playing at sword and dagger with a master of fence—three veneys for a dish of stewed prunes—[and I with my ward defending my head, he hot my shin,] and, by my troth, I cannot abide the smell of hot meat since....Why do your dogs bark so? be there 270
bears i'th' town?

Anne. I think there are, sir. I heard them talked of.

Slender. I love the sport well, but I shall as soon quarrel at it as any man in England...You are afraid, if you see the bear loose, are you not?

Anne. Ay, indeed, sir.

Slender. That's meat and drink to me, now: I have seen Sackerson loose—twenty times, and have taken him by the chain: but, I warrant you, the women have so cried and shrieked at it, that it passed...But women, indeed, 280
cannot abide 'em—they are very ill-favoured rough things.

PAGE opens the door

Page. Come, gentle Master Slender, come; we stay for you.

Slender. I'll eat nothing, I thank you, sir.

Page. By cock and pie, you shall not choose, sir: come, come! [*he stands aside to let him pass in*

Slender. Nay, pray you lead the way.

Page [*going in*]. Come on, sir.

Slender [*begins to follow but then turns*]. Mistress Anne...
290 yourself shall go first.

Anne. Not I, sir! pray you keep on.

Slender. Truly, I will not go first: truly, la! I will not do you that wrong.

Anne [*keeps behind him*]. I pray you, sir.

Slender. I'll rather be unmannerly than troublesome: you do yourself wrong, indeed, la!

He goes in; she follows after

[1. 2.] *Sir HUGH EVANS and SIMPLE appear at the door*

Evans. Go your ways, and ask of Doctor Caius' house which is the way; and there dwells one Mistress Quickly; which is in the manner of his nurse—or his dry nurse—or his cook—or his laundry—his washer and his wringer.

Simple. Well, sir.

Evans. Nay, it is petter yet...Give her this letter; for it is a 'oman, that altogether's acquaintance with Mistress Anne Page; and the letter is to desire and require her to solicit your master's desires to Mistress Anne Page: I pray
10 you, be gone...I will make an end of my dinner; there's pippins and seese to come.

SIMPLE departs; EVANS goes within

[1. 3.] *A room in the Garter Inn, hung with arras; stairs leading to a gallery.* FALSTAFF *seated at a table, drinking:* HOST *busy with mugs and pewter cans:* PISTOL, NYM, BARDOLPH *and* ROBIN

Falstaff [*sets down his cup of sack*]. Mine host of the Garter!

Host [*turns*]. What says my bully-rook? speak scholarly and wisely.

Falstaff. Truly, mine host; I must turn away some of my followers.

Host. Discard, bully Hercules, cashier; let them wag; trot, trot.

Falstaff. I sit at ten pounds a week.

Host. Thou'rt an emperor—Cæsar, Keisar, and Pheazar. 10
I will entertain Bardolph: he shall draw; he shall tap; said I well, bully Hector?

Falstaff. Do so, good mine host.

Host. I have spoke: let him follow...[*to Bardolph*] Let me see thee froth and lime: I am at a word: follow.
[*he goes out*

Falstaff. Bardolph, follow him: a tapster is a good trade: an old cloak makes a new jerkin: a withered serving-man a fresh tapster...Go, adieu.

Bardolph. It is a life that I have desired: I will thrive.

Pistol. O base Hungarian wight: wilt thou the spigot 20
wield? [*Bardolph follows Host*

Nym. He was gotten in drink. [His mind is not heroic, and there's the humour of it]...Is not the humour conceited?

Falstaff. I am glad I am so acquit of this tinderbox: his thefts were too open: his filching was like an unskilful singer, he kept not time.

Nym. The good humour is to steal at a [minim-rest.

Pistol. 'Convey,' the wise it call...'Steal!' foh! a fico
30 for the phrase.

Falstaff. Well, sirs, I am almost out at heels.

Pistol. Why, then, let kibes ensue.

Falstaff. There is no remedy: I must cony-catch, I must shift.

Pistol. Young ravens must have food.

Falstaff. Which of you know Ford of this town?

Pistol. I ken the wight: he is of substance good.

Falstaff. My honest lads, I will tell you what I am about.

Pistol. Two yards, and more.

40 *Falstaff.* No quips now, Pistol...Indeed, I am in the waist two yards about: but I am now about no waste: I am about thrift—Briefly: I do mean to make love to Ford's wife: I spy entertainment in her: she discourses: she carves: she gives the leer of invitation...I can construe the action of her familiar style, and the hardest voice of her behaviour—to be Englished rightly—is, 'I am Sir John Falstaff's.'

Pistol. He hath studied her †well, and translated her will...out of honesty into English.

50 *Nym.* The anchor is deep: will that humour pass?

Falstaff. Now, the report goes she has all the rule of her husband's purse: he hath a legion of angels.

Pistol. As many devils entertain! and 'To her, Boy,' say I.

Nym. The humour rises: it is good: humour me the angels.

Falstaff. I have writ me here a letter to her: and here another to Page's wife; who even now gave me good eyes too; examined my parts with most judicious œillades:
60 sometimes the beam of her view gilded my foot...sometimes my portly belly.

Pistol. Then did the sun on dunghill shine.

Nym. I thank thee for that humour.

Falstaff. O, she did so course o'er my exteriors with such a greedy intention, that the appetite of her eye did seem to scorch me up like a burning-glass...Here's another letter to her: she bears the purse too: she is a region in Guiana: all gold and bounty...I will be cheaters to them both, and they shall be exchequers to me: they shall be my East and West Indies, and I will trade to them both... 70
[*to Pistol*] Go, bear thou this letter to Mistress Page; [*to Nym*] and thou this to Mistress Ford: we will thrive, lads, we will thrive.

Pistol. Shall I Sir Pandarus of Troy become—
And by my side wear steel! then, Lucifer take all!

Nym. I will run no base humour: here, take the humour-letter; I will keep the haviour of reputation.

[*they throw the letters on the table*

Falstaff [*rising, to Robin*]. Hold, sirrah, bear you these letters tightly,
Sail like my pinnace to these golden shores....
Rogues, hence, avaunt, vanish like hail-stones; go!
Trudge; plod away i'th' hoof; seek shelter, pack... 80
Falstaff will learn the humour of the age,
French thrift, you rogues—myself and skirted page!

[*he sweeps out, with Robin following*

Pistol. Let vultures gripe thy guts: for gourd and fullam holds,
And high and low beguiles the rich and poor:
Tester I'll have in pouch when thou shalt lack,
Base Phrygian Turk!

Nym. I have operations [in my head] which be humours of revenge.

Pistol. Wilt thou revenge?

Nym. By welkin and her star! 90

Pistol. With wit or steel?

Nym. With both the humours, I:
I will discuss the humour of this love to Page.
Pistol. And I to Ford shall eke unfold,
How Falstaff, varlet vile,
His dove will prove, his gold will hold,
And his soft couch defile.
Nym. My humour shall not cool: I will incense Page to deal with poison: I will possess him with' †yellows, for the revolt of †mind is dangerous: that is my true humour.
100 *Pistol.* Thou art the Mars of malcontents: I second thee: troop on. [*they go*

[1. 4.] *A room in Doctor Caius' house: tables and shelves covered with books, papers, bottles, retorts etc.; a door at the back opening into a small closet; two other doors, one leading to the street, with a window beside it*

Mistress QUICKLY: SIMPLE

Quickly [*calling*]. What, John Rugby!

RUGBY *enters*

I pray thee, go to the casement, and see if you can see my master, Master Doctor Caius, coming: if he do, i'faith, and find any body in the house...here will be an old abusing of God's patience and the king's English.
Rugby. I'll go watch.
Quickly. Go, and we'll have a posset for't soon at night, in faith at the latter end of a sea-coal fire...[*Rugby goes to the window*] An honest, willing, kind fellow, as ever servant
10 shall come in house withal: and, I warrant you, no tell-tale nor no breed-bate: his worst fault is, that he is given to prayer; he is something peevish that way: but nobody but has his fault: but let that pass....Peter Simple, you say your name is?

Simple. Ay...for fault of a better.

Quickly. And Master Slender's your master?

Simple. Ay, forsooth.

Quickly. Does he not wear a great round beard, like a glover's paring-knife?

Simple. No, forsooth: he hath but a little †whey-face; with a little yellow beard...a cane-coloured beard. 20

Quickly. A softly-sprighted man, is he not?

Simple. Ay, forsooth: but he is as tall a man of his hands as any is between this and his head: he hath fought with a warrener!

Quickly. How say you?—O, I should remember him: does he not hold up his head, as it were, and strut in his gait?

Simple. Yes, indeed, does he.

Quickly. Well, heaven send Anne Page no worse fortune ...Tell Master Parson Evans I will do what I can for your master: Anne is a good girl, and I wish— 30

Rugby [*calls from the window*]. Out, alas! here comes my master.

Quickly. We shall all be shent...Run in here, good young man: go into this closet...[*she shuts Simple in the closet*] He will not stay long...[*calling*] What, John Rugby! John! what, John, I say!

CAIUS enters; she feigns not to see him

Go, John, go enquire for my master. I doubt he be not well, that he comes not home... [*she sings*

And down, down, adown-a, &c. 40

Caius [*suspicious*]. Vat is you sing? I do not like des toys: pray you, go and vetch me in my closet un boitier vert; a box, a green-a box...[*testily*] Do intend vat I speak? a green-a box. [*he busies himself with papers*

Quickly. Ay, forsooth, I'll fetch it you...[*to Rugby*] I am glad he went not in himself: if he had found the young man, he would have been horn mad. [*she goes to the closet*

Caius [*wipes his forehead*]. Fe, fe, fe, fe! ma foi, il fait fort chaud. Je m'en vais à la cour—la grande affaire.

50 *Quickly* [*returning with a green case*]. Is it this, sir?

Caius. Oui, mette le au mon pocket, dépêche Quickly... Vere is dat knave Rugby?

Quickly. What, John Rugby! John!

Rugby [*comes forward*]. Here, sir.

Caius. You are John Rugby, and you are Jack Rugby... Come, tak-a your rapier, and come after my heel to de court.

Rugby [*opening the door*]. 'Tis ready, sir, here in the porch.

60 *Caius* [*following swiftly*]. By my trot: I tarry too long ...[*stops*] Od's me...Qu'ai-j'oublié! [*rushes to the closet*] dere is some simples in my closet, dat I vill not for the varld I shall leave behind.

Quickly. Ay me, he'll find the young man there, and be mad.

Caius [*discovers Simple*]. O diable, diable! vat is in my closet? Villainy! laroon! [*pulling him out*] Rugby, my rapier.

Quickly. Good master, be content.

70 *Caius.* Verefore shall I be content-a?

Quickly. The young man is an honest man.

Caius. Vat shall de honest man do in my closet? dere is no honest man dat shall come in my closet.

Quickly. I beseech you, be not so phlegmatic: hear the truth of it....He came of an errand to me from Parson Hugh.

Caius. Vell.

Simple. Ay, forsooth...to desire her to—

Quickly. Peace, I pray you.

80 *Caius.* Peac-a your tongue...Speak-a your tale.

Simple. To desire this honest gentlewoman, your maid,

to speak a good word to Mistress Anne Page—for my master in the way of marriage.

Quickly. This is all, indeed, la! but I'll ne'er put my finger in the fire, and need not.

Caius. Sir Hugh send-a you! Rugby, baillez me some paper...tarry you a littl-a while.

[*he sits at his desk and writes*

Quickly [*draws Simple aside*]. I am glad he is so quiet: if he had been throughly moved, you should have heard him so loud, and so melancholy...But notwithstanding, 90 man, I'll do your master what good I can: and the very yea and the no is, the French doctor, my master—I may call him my master, look you, for I keep his house; and I wash, wring, brew, bake, scour, dress meat and drink, make the beds, and do all myself—

Simple. 'Tis a great charge to come under one body's hand.

Quickly. Are you avised o'that? you shall find it a great charge: and to be up early, and down late...but notwithstanding (to tell you in your ear, I would have no words 100 of it) my master himself is in love with Mistress Anne Page: but notwithstanding that I know Anne's mind, that's neither here nor there.

Caius [*rising and folding the letter*]. You, jack'nape! giv-a this letter to Sir Hugh. By gar, it is a shallenge: I vill cut his troat in de Park, and I vill teach a scurvy jack-a-nape priest to meddle or make!—You may be gone: it is not good you tarry here...[*Simple goes*] By gar, I vill cut all his two stones: by gar, he shall not have a stone to trow at his dog. 110

Quickly. Alas: he speaks but for his friend.

Caius [*turns upon her*]. It is no matter-a ver dat: do not you tell-a me dat I shall have Anne Page for myself? By gar, I vill kill de Jack-priest...and I have appointed mine host of de Jarteer to measure our weapon...by gar, I vill myself have Anne Page.

Quickly. Sir, the maid loves you, and all shall be well: We must give folks leave to prate...[*he boxes her ears*] What the good-jer! [*rubbing her head*

120 *Caius*. Rugby, come to the court vit me...[*to Quickly*] By gar, if I have not Anne Page, I shall turn your head out of my door...Follow my heels, Rugby.

Snatching up his green case and simples, he hurries out, followed by Rugby

Quickly. You shall have An—[*the door shuts*]—fool's-head of your own...No, I know Anne's mind for that: never a woman in Windsor knows more of Anne's mind than I do, nor can do more than I do with her, I thank heaven.

Fenton [*from outside*]. Who's within there, ho!

Quickly. Who's there, I trow? Come near the house, I pray you.

FENTON opens the door and enters

130 *Fenton*. How now, good woman, how dost thou?

Quickly. The better that it pleases your good worship to ask.

Fenton. What news? how does pretty Mistress Anne?

Quickly. In truth, sir, and she is pretty, and honest, and gentle, and one that is your friend, I can tell you that by the way, I praise heaven for it.

Fenton. Shall I do any good, think'st thou? Shall I not lose my suit?

Quickly. Troth, sir, all is in His hands above: but not-

140 withstanding, Master Fenton, I'll be sworn on a book she loves you...Have not your worship a wart above your eye?

Fenton. Yes marry have I, what of that?

Quickly. Well, thereby hangs a tale...good faith, it is

such another Nan; but—I detest—an honest maid as ever broke bread...We had an hour's talk of that wart; I shall never laugh but in that maid's company...but, indeed, she is given too much to allicholy and musing...But for you—well—go to—

Fenton. Well...I shall see her to-day: hold, there's money for thee...Let me have thy voice in my behalf: if thou seest her before me, commend me— 150

Quickly. Will I? i'faith, that we will: and I will tell your worship more of the wart the next time we have confidence, and of other wooers.

Fenton. Well, farewell. I am in great haste now.

[*he goes out*

Quickly. Farewell to your worship...Truly, an honest gentleman: but Anne loves him not: for I know Anne's mind as well as another does...Out upon't! what have I forgot? [*she hurries away* 160

[2. 1.] *The street before the house of Master Page*

Mistress PAGE, *in hat and muffler, comes forth with a letter in her hand*

Mistress Page. What, have I 'scaped love-letters in the holiday time of my beauty, and am I now a subject for them? Let me see! [*she reads*

'Ask me no reason why I love you, for though Love use Reason for his precisian, he admits him not for his councillor...You are not young, no more am I: go to then, there's sympathy...you are merry, so am I: ha! ha! then there's more sympathy...you love sack, and so do I: would you desire better sympathy? Let it suffice thee, Mistress Page, at the least if the love of a soldier can suffice, that 10 I love thee: I will not say, pity me—'tis not a soldier-like phrase; but I say, love me...

By me, thine own true knight, by day or night:
Or any kind of light, with all his might,
For thee to fight.
JOHN FALSTAFF.'

What a Herod of Jewry is this! O wicked, wicked world! One that is well-nigh worn to pieces with age to show himself a young gallant! What an unweighed behaviour 20 hath this Flemish drunkard picked (with the devil's name!) out of my conversation, that he dares in this manner assay me? Why, he hath not been thrice in my company: what should I say to him? I was then frugal of my mirth...Heaven forgive me! Why, I'll exhibit a bill in the parliament for the putting down of men...How shall I be revenged on him? for revenged I will be!—as sure as his guts are made of puddings.

Mistress FORD *appears, walking towards Page's house*

Mistress Ford. Mistress Page! trust me, I was going to your house.

30 *Mistress Page.* And, trust me, I was coming to you... You look very ill.

Mistress Ford. Nay, I'll ne'er believe that; I have to show to the contrary.

Mistress Page. Faith, but you do, in my mind.

Mistress Ford. Well: I do then: yet, I say, I could show you to the contrary...O Mistress Page, give me some counsel!

Mistress Page. What's the matter, woman?

Mistress Ford. O woman...if it were not for one trifling 40 respect, I could come to such honour.

Mistress Page. Hang the trifle, woman, take the honour: what is it? Dispense with trifles: what is it?

Mistress Ford. If I would but go to hell for an eternal moment or so...I could be knighted!

Mistress Page. What? thou liest! Sir Alice Ford! These knights will hack, and so thou shouldst not alter the article of thy gentry.

Mistress Ford. We burn day-light...[*hands her a letter*] Here, read, read: perceive how I might be knighted. I shall think the worse of fat men, as long as I have an eye 50 to make difference of men's liking: and yet he would not swear; praised women's modesty: and gave such orderly and well-behaved reproof to all uncomeliness, that I would have sworn his disposition would have gone to the truth of his words: but they do no more adhere and keep place together than the Hundredth Psalm to the tune of 'Green-sleeves'...What tempest, I trow, threw this whale, with so many tuns of oil in his belly, ashore at Windsor? How shall I be revenged on him? I think the best way were to entertain him with hope, till the wicked fire of lust have 60 melted him in his own grease...Did you ever hear the like?

Mistress Page [*holding the two letters, side by side*]. Letter for letter; but that the name of Page and Ford differs... To thy great comfort in this mystery of ill opinions, here's the twin-brother of thy letter: but let thine inherit first, for I protest mine never shall: I warrant he hath a thousand of these letters, writ with blank space for different names—sure more!—and these are of the second edition: he will print them out of doubt; for he cares not what he puts into the press, when he would put us two... 70 I had rather be a giantess, and lie under Mount Pelion... Well; I will find you twenty lascivious turtles ere one chaste man.

Mistress Ford [*taking Mistress Page's letter*]. Why, this is the very same...the very hand...the very words! What doth he think of us?

Mistress Page. Nay, I know not: it makes me almost ready to wrangle with mine own honesty: I'll entertain

myself like one that I am not acquainted withal; for, sure,
80 unless he know some strain in me, that I know not myself, he would never have boarded me in this fury.

Mistress Ford. 'Boarding,' call you it? I'll be sure to keep him above deck.

Mistress Page. So will I: if he come under my hatches, I'll never to sea again...Let's be revenged on him: let's appoint him a meeting; give him a show of comfort in his suit, and lead him on with a fine-baited delay, till he hath pawned his horses to mine host of the Garter.

Mistress Ford. Nay, I will consent to act any villainy
90 against him, that may not sully the chariness of our honesty...O, that my husband saw this letter: it would give eternal food to his jealousy.

Mistress Page. Why, look where he comes; and my good man too: he's as far from jealousy, as I am from giving him cause—and that, I hope, is an unmeasurable distance.

Mistress Ford. You are the happier woman.

Mistress Page. Let's consult together against this greasy knight...Come hither.

They seat themselves unseen under the trees, within earshot: FORD *and* PISTOL, PAGE *and* NYM *come up in pairs, talking*

Ford. Well...I hope it be not so.

100 *Pistol.* Hope is a curtal-dog in some affairs:
Sir John affects thy wife.

Ford. Why, sir, my wife is not young.

Pistol. He wooes both high and low, both rich and poor,
Both young and old, one with another, Ford.
He loves the gallimaufry—Ford, perpend.

Ford. Love my wife!

Pistol. With liver burning hot: prevent...or go thou,
†Like Sir Actæon be, with Ringwood at thy heels...
O, odious is the name!

Ford. What name, sir? 110

Pistol. The horn, I say...Farewell...
Take heed, have open eye, for thieves do foot by night....
Take heed, ere summer comes or cuckoo-birds do sing....
†Away, Sir Corporal Nym...[*to Page*] Believe it, he speaks sense. [*Pistol swaggers off*

Ford. I will be patient...I will find out this.

Nym [*to Page*]. And this is true: I like not the humour of lying: he hath wronged me in some humours: I should have borne the humoured letter to her: but I have a sword: and it shall bite upon my necessity: he loves your wife; there's the short and the long... 120
My name is Corporal Nym: I speak, and I avouch;
'Tis true: my name is Nym: and Falstaff loves your wife
...Adieu. I love not the humour of bread and cheese,
[and there's the humour of it]...Adieu.

[*he follows Pistol; Page and Ford muse apart*

Page. 'The humour of it,' quoth 'a! here's a fellow frights English out of his wits.

Ford. I will seek out Falstaff.

Page. I never heard such a drawling, affecting rogue.

Ford. If I do find it...well.

Page. I will not believe such a Cataian, though the 130 priest o'th' town commended him for a true man.

Ford. 'Twas a good sensible fellow...well.

Mistress PAGE *and Mistress* FORD *come forward, having heard all*

Page. How now, Meg!

Mistress Page. Whither go you, George? Hark you. [*they speak together*

Mistress Ford [*demure*]. How now, sweet Frank! why art thou melancholy?

Ford [*starts*]. I melancholy? I am not melancholy...Get you home: go. [*he turns away*

Mistress Ford. Faith, thou hast some crotchets in thy
140 head now...Will you go, Mistress Page?

Mistress Page. Have with you....You'll come to dinner, George? [*in Mistress Ford's ear*] Look, who comes yonder: she shall be our messenger to this paltry knight.

Mistress Ford. Trust me, I thought on her: she'll fit it.

Mistress QUICKLY *comes up*

Mistress Page. You are come to see my daughter Anne?

Quickly. Ay, forsooth: and, I pray, how does good Mistress Anne?

Mistress Page. Go in with us and see: we have an hour's talk with you. [*they go within*

150 *Page.* How now, Master Ford!

Ford [*rouses*]. You heard what this knave told me, did you not?

Page. Yes, and you heard what the other told me?

Ford. Do you think there is truth in them?

Page. Hang 'em, slaves: I do not think the knight would offer it: but these that accuse him in his intent towards our wives are a yoke of his discarded men...very rogues, now they be out of service.

Ford. Were they his men?

160 *Page.* Marry, were they.

Ford. I like it never the better for that. Does he lie at the Garter?

Page. Ay, marry, does he...If he should intend this voyage towards my wife, I would turn her loose to him; and what he gets more of her than sharp words, let it lie on my head.

Ford. I do not misdoubt my wife...but I would be loath to turn them together...a man may be too confident...I would have nothing lie on my head...I cannot be thus satisfied. 170

Host approaches in haste; Shallow following at a distance

Page. Look where my ranting host of the Garter comes: there is either liquor in his pate, or money in his purse, when he looks so merrily...How now, mine host!

Host. How now, bully-rook! thou'rt a gentleman. [*turns and calls*] Cavaliero-justice, I say!

Shallow [*breathless*]. I follow, mine host, I follow.... Good even and twenty, good Master Page! Master Page, will you go with us? we have sport in hand.

Host. Tell him, cavaliero-justice: tell him, bully-rook.

Shallow. Sir, there is a fray to be fought, between Sir 180 Hugh the Welsh priest and Caius the French doctor.

Ford. Good mine host o'th' Garter...a word with you.

Host. What sayst thou, my bully-rook?

[*they talk together apart*

Shallow [*to Page*]. Will you go with us to behold it? My merry host hath had the measuring of their weapons; and, I think, hath appointed them contrary places: for, believe me, I hear the parson is no jester: hark, I will tell you what our sport shall be.

[*they talk together apart*

Host. Hast thou no suit against my knight, my guest-cavalier? 190

†*Ford.* None, I protest: but I'll give you a pottle of burnt sack to give me recourse to him, and tell him my name is Brook...only for a jest.

Host. My hand, bully: thou shalt have egress and regress—said I well?—and thy name shall be Brook....It is a merry knight: Will you go, †Ameers? [*going*

Shallow. Have with you, mine host.

Page. I have heard the Frenchman hath good skill in his rapier.

200 *Shallow.* Tut, sir! I could have told you more: in these times you stand on distance...your passes, stoccadoes, and I know not what...'tis the heart, Master Page—'tis here, 'tis here: I have seen the time, with my long sword I would have made you four tall fellows skip like rats.

Host [*calling*]. Here, boys, here, here! shall we wag?

Page. Have with you...I had rather hear them scold than fight. [*Shallow and Page follow Host*

Ford. Though Page be a secure fool, and stands so firmly on his wife's frailty—yet I cannot put off my

210 opinion so easily: she was in his company at Page's house...and, what they made there, I know not....Well, I will look further into't, and I have a disguise to sound Falstaff...If I find her honest, I lose not my labour: if she be otherwise, 'tis labour well bestowed. [*he goes*

[2. 2.] *The room in the Garter Inn*

FALSTAFF: PISTOL

[*Pistol.* I will retort the sum in equipage.]

Falstaff. I will not lend thee a penny.

Pistol. Why, then the world's mine oyster,
Which I with sword will open.

Falstaff. Not a penny: I have been content, sir, you should lay my countenance to pawn: I have grated upon my good friends for three reprieves for you and your coach-fellow, Nym; or else you had looked through the grate, like a geminy of baboons: I am damned in hell for

10 swearing to gentlemen my friends, you were good soldiers and tall fellows....and when Mistress Bridget lost the handle of her fan, I took't upon mine honour thou hadst it not.

Pistol. Didst thou not share? hadst thou not fifteen pence?

Falstaff. Reason, you rogue, reason: think'st thou I'll endanger my soul gratis? At a word, hang no more about me, I am no gibbet for you...Go—a short knife and a throng—to your manor of Pickt-hatch...Go. You'll not bear a letter for me, you rogue! you stand upon your honour! why, thou unconfinable baseness, it is as much as I can do, to keep the terms of my honour precise...Ay, ay, I myself sometimes, leaving the fear of God on the left hand, and hiding mine honour in my necessity, am fain to shuffle, to hedge, and to lurch—and yet you, rogue, will ensconce your rags, your cat-a-mountain looks, your red-lattice phrases, and your †bold-beating oaths, under the shelter of your honour! You will not do it? you! 20

Pistol. I do relent: what wouldst thou more of man?

ROBIN enters

Robin. Sir, here's a woman would speak with you.

Falstaff. Let her approach.

Mistress QUICKLY enters simpering: ROBIN and PISTOL converse apart

Quickly [*curtsies*]. Give your worship good-morrow. 30

Falstaff. Good-morrow, good wife.

Quickly. Not so, an't please your worship.

Falstaff. Good maid, then.

Quickly. I'll be sworn,
As my mother was, the first hour I was born.

Falstaff. I do believe the swearer; what with me?

Quickly. Shall I vouchsafe your worship a word or two?

Falstaff. Two thousand—fair woman—and I'll vouchsafe thee the hearing. 40

Quickly. There is one Mistress Ford—[*glances round at Pistol and Robin*] Sir, I pray, come a little nearer this ways...I myself dwell with Master Doctor Caius...

Falstaff. Well, on; Mistress Ford, you say—

Quickly. Your worship says very true: I pray your worship, come a little nearer this ways.

Falstaff. I warrant thee, nobody hears: [*waves his hand towards Pistol and Robin*] mine own people, mine own people.

50 *Quickly*. Are they so? God bless them, and make them his servants!

Falstaff. Well; Mistress Ford, what of her?

Quickly. Why, sir; she's a good creature; Lord, Lord! your worship's a wanton...well...God forgive you, and all of us, I pray—

Falstaff. Mistress Ford...come, Mistress Ford.

Quickly. Marry, this is the short and the long of it: you have brought her into such a canaries, as 'tis wonderful: the best courtier of them all (when the court lay at
60 Windsor) could never have brought her to such a canary: yet there has been knights, and lords, and gentlemen, with their coaches; I warrant you, coach after coach, letter after letter, gift after gift; smelling so sweetly, all musk, and so rushling, I warrant you, in silk and gold, and in such alligant terms, and in such wine and sugar of the best, and the fairest, that would have won any woman's heart: and, I warrant you, they could never get an eye-wink of her: I had myself twenty angels given me this morning, but I defy all angels—in any such sort, as
70 they say—but in the way of honesty: and, I warrant you, they could never get her so much as sip on a cup with the proudest of them all, and yet there has been earls... nay, which is more, pensioners—but, I warrant you, all is one with her.

Falstaff. But what says she to me? be brief, my good she-Mercury.

Quickly. Marry, she hath received your letter: for the which she thanks you a thousand times; and she gives you to notify that her husband will be absence from his house between ten and eleven. 80

Falstaff. Ten and eleven?

Quickly. Ay, forsooth: and then you may come and see the picture, she says, that you wot of: Master Ford, her husband, will be from home: alas! the sweet woman leads an ill life with him: he's a very jealousy man; she leads a very frampold life with him—good heart!

Falstaff. Ten and eleven....Woman, commend me to her. I will not fail her.

Quickly. Why, you say well...But I have another messenger to your worship: Mistress Page hath her hearty 90 commendations to you, too: and let me tell you in your ear, she's as fartuous a civil modest wife, and one, I tell you, that will not miss you morning nor evening prayer, as any is in Windsor, whoe'er be the other: and she bade me tell your worship that her husband is seldom from home, but she hopes there will come a time....I never knew a woman so dote upon a man; surely, I think you have charms, la...yes, in truth.

Falstaff. Not I, I assure thee; setting the attraction of my good parts aside, I have no other charms. 100

Quickly. Blessing on your heart for't!

Falstaff. But I pray thee tell me this: has Ford's wife, and Page's wife, acquainted each other how they love me?

Quickly. That were a jest, indeed! they have not so little grace, I hope—that were a trick, indeed! But Mistress Page would desire you to send her your little page, of all loves: her husband has a marvellous infection to the little page: and, truly, Master Page is an honest

man: never a wife in Windsor leads a better life than she
110 does: do what she will, say what she will, take all, pay all, go to bed when she list, rise when she list, all is as she will: and, truly, she deserves it; for if there be a kind woman in Windsor, she is one: you must send her your page—no remedy.

Falstaff. Why, I will.

Quickly. Nay, but do so then—and, look you, he may come and go between you both: and, in any case, have a nay-word, that you may know one another's mind, and the boy never need to understand any thing; for 'tis not
120 good that children should know any wickedness: old folks, you know, have discretion, as they say, and know the world.

Falstaff. Fare thee well. Commend me to them both: there's my purse—I am yet thy debtor...Boy, go along with this woman. [*Quickly and Robin go out*] This news distracts me....

(*Pistol*. †This pink is one of Cupid's carriers—
Clap on more sails, pursue: up with your fights:
Give fire: she is my prize, or ocean whelm them all!
[*he pursues them*

130 *Falstaff*. Sayst thou so, old Jack? go thy ways: I'll make more of thy old body than I have done: will they yet look after thee? wilt thou, after the expense of so much money, be now a gainer? Good body, I thank thee: let them say 'tis grossly done—so it be fairly done, no matter.

BARDOLPH *enters, with a cup of sack*

Bardolph. Sir John, there's one Master Brook below would fain speak with you, and be acquainted with you; and hath sent your worship a morning's draught of sack.

Falstaff. Brook is his name?

Bardolph. Ay, sir.

Falstaff. Call him in...[*Bardolph goes out*] Such Brooks 140
are welcome to me, that o'erflow such liquor...[*he drains the cup*] Ah, ha! Mistress Ford and Mistress Page, have I encompassed you? go to, via!

BARDOLPH returns, with FORD disguised carrying a bag of money

Ford. Bless you, sir.

Falstaff. And you, sir: would you speak with me?

Ford. I make bold, to press with so little preparation upon you.

Falstaff. You're welcome. What's your will? Give us leave, drawer. [*Bardolph leaves them*

Ford. Sir, I am a gentleman that have spent much. 150
My name is Brook.

Falstaff. Good Master Brook, I desire more acquaintance of you.

Ford. Good Sir John, I sue for yours: not to charge you, for I must let you understand I think myself in better plight for a lender than you are: the which hath something emboldened me to this unseasoned intrusion: for they say, if money go before, all ways do lie open.

Falstaff. Money is a good soldier, sir, and will on.

Ford. Troth, and I have a bag of money here troubles 160
me: if you will help me to bear it, Sir John, take all, or half, for easing me of the carriage.

Falstaff. Sir, I know not how I may deserve to be your porter.

Ford. I will tell you, sir, if you will give me the hearing.

Falstaff. Speak, good Master Brook. I shall be glad to be your servant.

Ford. Sir, I hear you are a scholar—I will be brief with you—and you have been a man long known to me, though I had never so good means, as desire, to make myself 170 acquainted with you....I shall discover a thing to you, wherein I must very much lay open mine own imperfection: but, good Sir John, as you have one eye upon my follies, as you hear them unfolded, turn another into the register of your own, that I may pass with a reproof the easier, sith you yourself know how easy it is to be such an offender.

Falstaff. Very well, sir. Proceed.

Ford. There is a gentlewoman in this town—her
180 husband's name is Ford.

Falstaff. Well, sir.

Ford. I have long loved her, and, I protest to you, bestowed much on her: followed her with a doting observance; engrossed opportunities to meet her; fee'd every slight occasion that could but niggardly give me sight of her; not only bought many presents to give her, but have given largely to many to know what she would have given: briefly, I have pursued her, as love hath pursued me, which hath been on the wing of all occasions...
190 but whatsoever I have merited—either in my mind or in my means—meed, I am sure, I have received none, unless experience be a jewel. That I have purchased at an infinite rate, and that hath taught me to say this—
"Love like a shadow flies when substance love pursues,
"Pursuing that that flies, and flying what pursues."

Falstaff. Have you received no promise of satisfaction at her hands?

Ford. Never.

Falstaff. Have you importuned her to such a purpose?

200 *Ford.* Never.

Falstaff. Of what quality was your love, then?

Ford. Like a fair house built upon another man's ground—so that I have lost my edifice by mistaking the place where I erected it.

Falstaff. To what purpose have you unfolded this to me?

Ford. When I have told you that, I have told you all... Some say, that though she appear honest to me, yet in other places she enlargeth her mirth so far that there is shrewd construction made of her....Now, Sir John, here is the heart of my purpose: you are a gentleman of excellent breeding, admirable discourse, of great admittance, authentic in your place and person, generally allowed for your many war-like, court-like, and learned preparations. 210

Falstaff. O, sir!

Ford. Believe it, for you know it...[*he places the bag on the table*]There is money. Spend it, spend it, spend more; spend all I have, only give me so much of your time in exchange of it, as to lay an amiable siege to the honesty of this Ford's wife: use your art of wooing; win her to consent to you: if any man may, you may as soon as any. 220

Falstaff. Would it apply well to the vehemency of your affection, that I should win what you would enjoy? Methinks you prescribe to yourself very preposterously.

Ford. O, understand my drift: she dwells so securely on the excellency of her honour, that the folly of my soul dares not present itself; she is too bright to be looked against....Now, could I come to her with any detection in my hand...my desires had instance and argument to commend themselves. I could drive her then from the ward of her purity, her reputation, her marriage-vow, and a thousand other her defences, which now are too-too strongly embattled against me: what say you to't, Sir John? 230

Falstaff [*weighing the bag in his hand*]. Master Brook, I will first make bold with your money; next, give me your hand; and last, as I am a gentleman, you shall, if you will, enjoy Ford's wife.

Ford. O good sir!

Falstaff. I say you shall.

Ford. Want no money, Sir John, you shall want none.

240 *Falstaff.* Want no Mistress Ford, Master Brook, you shall want none: I shall be with her—I may tell you—by her own appointment. Even as you came in to me, her assistant, or go-between, parted from me: I say I shall be with her between ten and eleven; for at that time the jealous rascally knave, her husband, will be forth...Come you to me at night, you shall know how I speed.

Ford [*bowing*]. I am blest in your acquaintance...Do you know Ford, sir?

Falstaff. Hang him, poor cuckoldly knave! I know him 250 not: yet I wrong him to call him poor: they say the jealous wittolly knave hath masses of money, for the which his wife seems to me well-favoured: I will use her as the key of the cuckoldly rogue's coffer—and there's my harvest-home.

Ford. I would you knew Ford, sir, that you might avoid him, if you saw him.

Falstaff. Hang him, mechanical salt-butter rogue! I will stare him out of his wits: I will awe him with my cudgel: it shall hang like a meteor o'er the cuckold's horns...

260 Master Brook, thou shalt know, I will predominate over the peasant, and thou shalt lie with his wife....Come to me soon at night: Ford's a knave, and I will aggravate his style: thou, Master Brook, shalt know him for knave—and cuckold....Come to me soon at night.

[*he takes up the bag and goes*

Ford. What a damned Epicurean rascal is this! My heart is ready to crack with impatience...Who says this is improvident jealousy? my wife hath sent to him, the hour is fixed, the match is made...Would any man have thought this? See the hell of having a false woman: my

270 bed shall be abused, my coffers ransacked, my reputation gnawn at, and I shall not only receive this villainous

wrong, but stand under the adoption of abominable terms, and by him that does me this wrong...Terms, names! Amaimon sounds well; Lucifer, well; Barbason, well; yet they are devils' additions, the names of fiends: but Cuckold! Wittol!—Cuckold! the devil himself hath not such a name....Page is an ass, a secure ass; he will trust his wife, he will not be jealous: I will rather trust a Fleming with my butter, Parson Hugh the Welshman with my cheese, an Irishman with my aqua-vitæ bottle, 280
or a thief to walk my ambling gelding, than my wife with herself....Then she plots, then she ruminates, then she devises: and what they think in their hearts they may effect, they will break their hearts but they will effect.... God be praised for my jealousy...Eleven o'clock the hour. I will prevent this, detect my wife, be revenged on Falstaff, and laugh at Page....I will about it—better three hours too soon, than a minute too late....Fie, fie, fie! cuckold! cuckold! cuckold! [*he rushes from the room*

[2. 3.] *A field near Windsor*

CAIUS and RUGBY, walking to and fro

Caius [*stops*]. Jack Rugby!

Rugby. Sir.

Caius. Vat is de clock, Jack?

Rugby. 'Tis past the hour, sir, that Sir Hugh promised to meet.

Caius. By gar, he has save his soul, dat he is no-come: he has pray his Pible well, dat he is no-come: by gar, Jack Rugby, he is dead already, if he be come.

Rugby. He is wise, sir: he knew your worship would kill him if he came. 10

Caius. By gar, de herring is no dead, so as I vill kill him ...Take your rapier, Jack! I vill tell you how I vill kill him.

Rugby. Alas, sir, I cannot fence.
Caius. Villainy, take your rapier. [*they begin to fence*
Rugby. Forbear...here's company.

HOST, SHALLOW, SLENDER, and PAGE come up

Host. Bless thee, bully doctor.
Shallow. Save you, Master Doctor Caius.
Page. Now, good master doctor!
Slender. Give you good-morrow, sir.
20 *Caius.* Vat be all you, one, two, tree, four, come for?
Host. To see thee fight, to see thee foin, to see thee traverse, to see thee here, to see thee there, to see thee pass thy punto, thy stock, thy reverse, thy distance, thy montánt...Is he dead, my Ethiopian? is he dead, my Francisco? ha, bully! What says my Æsculapius? my Galen? my heart of elder? Ha! is he dead, bully-stale? is he dead?
Caius. By gar, he is de Coward-Jack-Priest of de vorld: he is not show his face.
30 *Host.* Thou art a Castilian-King-Urinal! Hector of Greece, my boy!
Caius. I pray you, bear vitness that me have stay six or seven, two, tree hours for him, and he is no-come.
Shallow. He is the wiser man, master doctor! he is a curer of souls, and you a curer of bodies: if you should fight, you go against the hair of your professions: is it not true, Master Page?
Page. Master Shallow...you have yourself been a great fighter, though now a man of peace.
40 *Shallow.* Bodykins, Master Page, though I now be old, and of the peace...if I see a sword out, my finger itches to make one...Though we are justices, and doctors, and churchmen, Master Page, we have some salt of our youth in us—we are the sons of women, Master Page.

Page. 'Tis true, Master Shallow.

Shallow. It will be found so, Master Page...Master Doctor Caius, I am come to fetch you home...I am sworn of the peace: you have showed yourself a wise physician, and Sir Hugh hath shown himself a wise and patient churchman...You must go with me, master doctor. 50

Host. Pardon, guest-justice...a [word,] Mounseur †Mock-water.

Caius. Mock-vater? vat is dat?

Host. Mock-water, in our English tongue, is valour, bully.

Caius. By gar, then I have as much mock-vater as de Englishman...scurvy jack-dog priest! by gar, me vill cut his ears.

Host. He will clapper-claw thee tightly, bully. 60

Caius. Clapper-de-claw! vat is dat?

Host. That is, he will make thee amends.

Caius. By gar, me do look he shall clapper-de-claw me—for, by gar, me vill have it.

Host. And I will provoke him to't, or let him wag.

Caius. Me tank you for dat.

Host. And moreover, bully,—[*aside*] But first, master guest, and Master Page, and eke Cavaliero Slender, go you through the town to Frogmore.

(*Page.* Sir Hugh is there, is he? 70

(*Host.* He is there. See what humour he is in; and I will bring the doctor about by the fields: will it do well?

(*Shallow.* We will do it.

Page, Shallow, Slender. Adieu, good master doctor. [*they depart*

Caius. By gar, me vill kill de priest, for he speak for a jack-an-ape to Anne Page.

Host. Let him die: [but, first,] sheathe thy impatience;

throw cold water on thy choler: go about the fields with me through Frogmore. I will bring thee where Mistress
80 Anne Page is, at a farm-house a-feasting; and thou shalt woo her...Cried-game, said I well?

Caius. By gar, me dank you vor dat: by gar, I love you; and I shall procur-a you de good guest: de earl, de knight, de lords, de gentlemen, my patients.

Host. For the which, I will be thy adversary toward Anne Page: said I well?

Caius. By gar, 'tis good: vell said.

Host. Let us wag then.

Caius. Come at my heels, Jack Rugby. [*they go off*

[3. 1.] *A meadow near Frogmore, with a field-path and two stiles, one hard-by, the other at a distance: Sir* HUGH EVANS, *in doublet and hose; a drawn sword in one hand and an open book in the other.* SIMPLE *on the look-out up a tree*

Evans [*calls*]. I pray you now, good Master Slender's serving-man, and friend Simple by your name, which way have you looked for Master Caius, that calls himself doctor of physic?

Simple. Marry, sir, the †pittie-ward, the park-ward, every way: old Windsor way, and every way but the town way.

Evans. I most fehemently desire you, you will also look that way.

10 *Simple.* I will, sir.

Evans. Pless my soul! how full of cholers I am, and trempling of mind...I shall be glad, if he have deceived me...how melancholies I am!—I will knog his urinals about his knave's costard, when I have goot opportunities for the 'ork...Pless my soul! [*he sings*

To shallow rivers, to whose falls:
Melodious birds sing madrigals:
There will we make our peds of roses:
And a thousand fragrant posies....
To shallow— 20

Mercy on me! I have a great dispositions to cry....
Melodious birds sing madrigals— [*he sings again*
When as I sat in Pabylon
And a thousand vagram posies....
To shallow, etc.—

Simple [*descending the tree*]. Yonder he is coming, this way, Sir Hugh.

Evans. He's welcome...[*sings*] To shallow rivers, to whose falls...Heaven prosper the right...What weapons is he?

Simple. No weapons, sir...[*points*] There comes my 30 master, Master Shallow, and another gentleman; from Frogmore, over the stile, this way.

Evans. Pray you, give me my gown—or else keep it in your arms. [*Simple takes up the gown from the ground*

PAGE and SHALLOW come over the near stile, with SLENDER following. At the same time HOST, CAIUS and RUGBY are seen climbing the stile afar off

Shallow. How now, master parson! Good-morrow, good Sir Hugh...Keep a gamester from the dice, and a good student from his book, and it is wonderful.

Slender [*sighs*]. Ah, sweet Anne Page.

Page. Save you, good Sir Hugh.

Evans. Got-pless you from his mercy sake, all of you 40

Shallow. What! the Sword and the Word! do you study them both, master parson?

Page. And youthful still, in your doublet and hose, this raw rheumatic day?

Evans. There is reasons and causes for it.

Page. We are come to you, to do a good office, master parson.

Evans. Fery well: what is it?

Page [*looking over Evans' shoulder*]. Yonder is a most
50 reverend gentleman; who belike, having received wrong by some person, is at most odds with his own gravity and patience that ever you saw.

Shallow. I have lived fourscore years and upward: I never heard a man of his place, gravity, and learning, so wide of his own respect.

Evans. What is he? [*Host, Caius and Rugby approach*

Page. I think you know him...[*Evans turns*] Master Doctor Caius, the renowned French physician!

Evans. Got's will, and his passion of my heart! I had
60 as lief you would tell me of a mess of porridge.

Page. Why?

Evans. He has no more knowledge in Hibocrates and Galen—[*raises his voice*] and he is a knave besides: a cowardly knave as you would desires to be acquainted withal. [*Caius runs forward with rapier and dagger drawn*

Page. I warrant you, he's the man should fight with him.

Slender [*sighs*]. O, sweet Anne Page!

Shallow. It appears so, by his weapons...Keep them
70 asunder...Here comes Doctor Caius! [*he crosses his path*

Page [*steps in front of Evans*]. Nay, good master parson, keep in your weapon.

Shallow. So do you, good master doctor.

Host. Disarm them, and let them question: let them keep their limbs whole, and hack our English.

[*they are disarmed*

Caius. I pray you, let-a me speak a word with your ear; Verefore vill you not meet-a me?

Evans. Pray you, use your patience in good time.

Caius. By gar, you are de coward...de Jack-dog... John ape. 80

(*Evans.* Pray you, let us not be laughing-stogs to other men's humours: I desire you in friendship, and I will one way or other make you amends...
[*aloud*] I will knog your urinals about your knave's cogscomb, [for missing your meetings and appointments!]

Caius. Diable...Jack Rugby...mine host de Jarteer... have I not stay for him, to kill him? have I not, at de place I did appoint?

Evans. As I am a Christians-soul, now look you: this is the place appointed—I'll be judgement by mine host of 90 the Garter.

Host. Peace, I say, Gallia and Gaul, French and Welsh, soul-curer and body-curer.

Caius. Ay, dat is very good! excellent!

Host. Peace, I say; hear mine host of the Garter. Am I politic? am I subtle? am I a Machiavel? Shall I lose my doctor? no—he gives me the potions and the motions.... Shall I lose my parson? my priest? my Sir Hugh? no— he gives me the proverbs and the no-verbs....[Give me thy hand, terrestrial; so...] Give me thy hand, celestial; 100 so...[*joins their hands*] Boys of art, I have deceived you both: I have directed you to wrong places: your hearts are mighty, your skins are whole, and let burnt sack be the issue...[*to Page and Shallow*] Come, lay their swords to pawn...Follow me, lads of peace—follow, follow, follow.

[*he mounts the stile*

Shallow. Trust me, a mad host...Follow, gentlemen, follow.

Slender [*sighs*]. O, sweet Anne Page!

[*Shallow, Page and Slender follow Host*

Caius. Ha! do I perceive dat? have you mak-a de sot of us? ha, ha! 110

Evans. This is well! he has made us his vlouting-stog... I desire you that we may be friends: and let us knog our prains together to be revenge on this same scall, scurvy, cogging companion, the host of the Garter.

Caius. By gar, with all my heart: he promise to bring me where is Anne Page: by gar, he deceive me too.

Evans. Well, I will smite his noddles...Pray you, follow.

[*they climb the stile*

[3. 2.] *A street in Windsor, near the house of Master Ford*

Mistress PAGE *approaches with* ROBIN *strutting before her; he pauses*

Mistress Page. Nay, keep your way, little gallant; you were wont to be a follower, but now you are a leader... Whether had you rather, lead mine eyes or eye your master's heels?

Robin. I had rather, forsooth, go before you like a man than follow him like a dwarf.

Mistress Page. O you are a flattering boy. Now, I see, you'll be a courtier.

FORD *comes up the street.*

Ford. Well met, Mistress Page....Whither go you?

10 *Mistress Page.* Truly, sir, to see your wife. Is she at home?

Ford. Ay—and as idle as she may hang together, for want of company: I think, if your husbands were dead, you two would marry.

Mistress Page. Be sure of that—two other husbands.

Ford. Where had you this pretty weathercock?

Mistress Page. I cannot tell what the dickens his name is my husband had him of. What do you call your knight's name, sirrah?

20 *Robin.* Sir John Falstaff.

Ford. Sir John Falstaff!

Mistress Page. He, he—I can never hit on's name; there is such a league between my good man and he! Is your wife at home, indeed?

Ford. Indeed she is.

Mistress Page [*curtsies*]. By your leave, sir. I am sick, till I see her. [*she hurries on, with Robin before her*

Ford. Has Page any brains? hath he any eyes? hath he any thinking? Sure, they sleep—he hath no use of them... Why, this boy will carry a letter twenty mile as easy—as 30 a cannon will shoot point blank twelve score! He pieces out his wife's inclination; he gives her folly motion and advantage: and now she's going to my wife, and Falstaff's boy with her...A man may hear this shower sing in the wind...and Falstaff's boy with her...good plots, they are laid, and our revolted wives share damnation together... Well, I will take him, then torture my wife, pluck the borrowed veil of modesty from the so-seeming Mistress Page, divulge Page himself for a secure and wilful Actæon—and to these violent proceedings all my neighbours shall cry aim.... 40 [*the town-clock strikes*] The clock gives me my cue, and my assurance bids me search—there I shall find Falstaff...I shall be rather praised for this than mocked; for it is as positive as the earth is firm that Falstaff is there...I will go.

Turning, he meets PAGE, SHALLOW, SLENDER, HOST, *Sir* HUGH EVANS, CAIUS, *and* RUGBY *coming up the street*

All. Well met, Master Ford.

Ford. Trust me, a good knot; I have good cheer at home, and I pray you all go with me.

Shallow. I must excuse myself, Master Ford.

Slender. And so must I, sir. We have appointed to dine with Mistress Anne, and I would not break with her for 50 more money than I'll speak of.

Shallow. We have lingered about a match between Anne Page and my cousin Slender, and this day we shall have our answer.

Slender. I hope I have your good will, father Page.

Page. You have, Master Slender. I stand wholly for you—but my wife, master doctor, is for you altogether.

Caius. Ay, be-gar, and de maid is lov-a me: my nursh-a Quickly tell me so mush.

60 *Host.* What say you to young Master Fenton? he capers, he dances, he has eyes of youth...he writes verses, he speaks holiday, he smells April and May. He will carry't, he will carry't—'tis in his †buttons—he will carry't.

Page. Not by my consent, I promise you....The gentleman is of no having—he kept company with the wild Prince and Poins: he is of too high a region, he knows too much...No, he shall not knit a knot in his fortunes with the finger of my substance: if he take her, let him take her simply: the wealth I have waits on my consent, and
70 my consent goes not that way.

Ford. I beseech you, heartily, some of you go home with me to dinner: besides your cheer, you shall have sport—I will show you a monster! Master doctor, you shall go—so shall you, Master Page—and you, Sir Hugh.

Shallow. Well, fare you well: we shall have the freer wooing at Master Page's. [*he goes off with Slender*

Caius. Go home, John Rugby. I come anon.

[*Rugby obeys*

Host. Farewell, my hearts. I will to my honest knight Falstaff, and drink canary with him. [*he follows Rugby*

80 (*Ford.* I think I shall drink in pipe-wine first with him—I'll make him dance!

[*aloud*] Will you go, gentles?

Page, Caius, Evans. Have with you, to see this monster.

[*they go with Ford*

[3. 3.] *The hall of Master Ford's house, hung with arras; stairs leading to a gallery; a large open hearth; three doors, one with windows right and left opening into the street*

Mistress FORD *and Mistress* PAGE, *bustling*

Mistress Ford [*calls*]. What, John! what, Robert!
Mistress Page. Quickly, quickly...is the buck-basket—
Mistress Ford. I warrant....What, Robin, I say!

Two servants enter carrying a large basket

Mistress Page [*impatient*]. Come, come, come!
Mistress Ford. Here, set it down. [*they do so*
Mistress Page. Give your men the charge. We must be brief.
Mistress Ford. Marry, as I told you before, John and Robert, be ready here hard by in the brew-house, and when I suddenly call you, come forth, and—without any 10 pause or staggering—take this basket on your shoulders: that done, trudge with it in all haste, and carry it among the whitsters in Datchet-mead, and there empty it in the muddy ditch, close by the Thames side.
Mistress Page. You will do it?
Mistress Ford. I ha' told them over and over. They lack no direction....Be gone, and come when you are called. [*the servants go out; Robin enters*
Mistress Page. Here comes little Robin.
Mistress Ford. How now, my eyas-musket! what news 20 with you?
Robin. My master, Sir John, is come in at your back-door, Mistress Ford, and requests your company.
Mistress Page. You little Jack-a-lent, have you been true to us?

Robin. Ay, I'll be sworn...My master knows not of your being here: and hath threatened to put me into everlasting liberty, if I tell you of it; for he swears he'll turn me away.

30 *Mistress Page.* Thou'rt a good boy: this secrecy of thine shall be a tailor to thee, and shall make thee a new doublet and hose....I'll go hide me.

Mistress Ford. Do so...Go tell thy master, I am alone... [*he goes*] Mistress Page, remember you your cue.

Mistress Page. I warrant thee. If I do not act it, hiss me.

Mistress Ford. Go to then: we'll use this unwholesome humidity, this gross watery pumpion; we'll teach him to know turtles from jays.

Mistress PAGE *goes forth by one door, leaving it ajar;* FALSTAFF *enters by another*

40 *Falstaff.* 'Have I caught my heavenly jewel?'
Why, now let me die, for I have lived long enough...This is the period of my ambition...O this blessed hour!

Mistress Ford. O sweet Sir John! [*they embrace*

Falstaff. Mistress Ford, I cannot cog, I cannot prate, Mistress Ford. Now shall I sin in my wish; I would thy husband were dead. I'll speak it before the best lord, I would make thee my lady.

Mistress Ford. I your lady, Sir John! alas, I should be a pitiful lady.

50 *Falstaff.* Let the court of France show me such another: I see how thine eye would emulate the diamond: thou hast the right arched beauty of the brow that becomes the ship-tire, the tire-valiant, or any tire of Venetian admittance.

Mistress Ford. A plain kerchief, Sir John: my brows become nothing else—nor that well, neither.

Falstaff. Thou art a tyrant to say so: thou wouldst make an absolute courtier, and the firm fixture of thy foot would give an excellent motion to thy gait, in a semi-circled farthingale....I see what thou wert, if fortune thy 60 foe were not, nature thy friend...Come, thou canst not hide it.

Mistress Ford. Believe me, there's no such thing in me.

Falstaff. What made me love thee? let that persuade thee there's something extraordinary in thee...Come, I cannot cog and say thou art this and that, like a many of these lisping hawthorn-buds, that come like women in men's apparel, and smell like Bucklersbury in simple-time: I cannot—but I love thee, none but thee; and thou 70 deserv'st it.

Mistress Ford. Do not betray me, sir. I fear you love Mistress Page.

Falstaff. Thou mightst as well say, I love to walk by the Counter-gate, which is as hateful to me as the reek of a lime-kiln.

Mistress Ford. Well, heaven knows how I love you—[*with meaning*] and you shall one day find it.

Falstaff. Keep in that mind. I'll deserve it.

Mistress Ford. Nay, I must tell you, so you do; [*with* 80 *meaning*] or else I could not be in that mind.

ROBIN *enters, in haste*

Robin. Mistress Ford, Mistress Ford! here's Mistress Page at the door, sweating, and blowing, and looking wildly, and would needs speak with you presently.

Falstaff. She shall not see me. I will ensconce me behind the arras.

Mistress Ford. Pray you, do so—she's a very tattling woman.... [*Falstaff stands behind the arras*

Mistress PAGE *comes from her hiding-place*

What's the matter? how now!

90 *Mistress Page* [*seeming breathless*]. O Mistress Ford, what have you done? You're shamed, you're overthrown, you're undone for ever!

Mistress Ford. What's the matter, good Mistress Page?

Mistress Page. O well-a-day, Mistress Ford! having an honest man to your husband, to give him such cause of suspicion!

Mistress Ford. What cause of suspicion?

Mistress Page. What cause of suspicion! Out upon you! how am I mistook in you!

100 *Mistress Ford.* Why, alas, what's the matter?

Mistress Page. Your husband's coming hither, woman, with all the officers in Windsor, to search for a gentleman that he says is here now in the house—by your consent—to take an ill advantage of his absence...You are undone.

Mistress Ford. 'Tis not so, I hope.

Mistress Page. Pray heaven it be not so, that you have such a man here: but 'tis most certain your husband's coming, with half Windsor at his heels, to search for such

110 a one. I come before to tell you...If you know yourself clear, why I am glad of it: but if you have a friend here, convey, convey him out....Be not amazed, call all your senses to you, defend your reputation, or bid farewell to your good life for ever.

Mistress Ford. What shall I do? There is a gentleman, my dear friend: and I fear not mine own shame so much—as his peril....I had rather than a thousand pound, he were out of the house.

Mistress Page. For shame, never stand 'you had rather,'

120 and 'you had rather': your husband's here at hand!

Bethink you of some conveyance: in the house you cannot hide him....O, how have you deceived me! Look, here is a basket, if he be of any reasonable stature, he may creep in here—and throw foul linen upon him, as if it were going to bucking: or—it is whiting-time—send him by your two men to Datchet-mead.

Mistress Ford. He's too big to go in there: what shall I do?

FALSTAFF thrusting the arras aside, rushes towards the basket

Falstaff. Let me see't, let me see't, O let me see't...I'll in, I'll in...follow your friend's counsel—I'll in. 130

[*he plucks out the linen*

Mistress Page. What! Sir John Falstaff! [*in his ear*] Are these your letters, knight?

Falstaff [*climbing into the basket*]. I love thee, [and none but thee], help me away...let me creep in here... I'll never—

Voices heard in the street without; he crouches; they cover him with foul linen

Mistress Page. Help to cover your master, boy! Call your men, Mistress Ford....You dissembling knight!

Mistress Ford [*calling*]. What, John, Robert, John!

ROBIN hastily thrusts the remainder of the linen into the basket and runs off; the servants enter swiftly

Go take up these clothes here, quickly...Where's the cowl-staff? look, how you drumble...[*they pass a pole through the handles of the basket*] Carry them to the laundress in Datchet-mead...[*they hoist the basket, staggering*] quickly, come! 140

The door opens; FORD, PAGE, CAIUS, and Sir HUGH EVANS enter from the street

Ford. Pray you, come near: if I suspect without cause, why then make sport at me, then let me be your jest—I deserve it...How now! [who goes here?] whither bear you this?

Servants. To the laundress, forsooth.

Mistress Ford. Why, what have you to do whither they 150 bear it? You were best meddle with buck-washing.

Ford. Buck? I would I could wash myself of the buck! Buck, buck, buck! Ay, buck: I warrant you, buck—and of the season too it shall appear....[*the servants bear away the basket*] Gentlemen, I have dreamed to-night. I'll tell you my dream...Here, here, here be my keys. Ascend my chambers, search, seek, find out: I'll warrant we'll unkennel the fox....[*goes to the outer door*] Let me stop this way first...[*locks it*] So, now † untapis!

Page. Good Master Ford, be contented: you wrong 160 yourself too much.

Ford. True, Master Page. Up, gentlemen—you shall see sport anon...[*mounts the stairs*] Follow me, gentlemen. [*they hesitate*

Evans. This is fery fantastical humours and jealousies.

Caius. By gar, 'tis no the fashion of France: it is not jealous in France.

Page. Nay, follow him, gentlemen. See the issue of his search. [*they go up*

Mistress Page. Is there not a double excellency in this?

Mistress Ford. I know not which pleases me better, that 170 my husband is deceived, or Sir John.

Mistress Page. What a taking was he in, when your husband asked who was in the basket!

Mistress Ford. I am half afraid he will have need of

washing: so throwing him into the water will do him a benefit.

Mistress Page. Hang him, dishonest rascal...I would all of the same strain were in the same distress.

Mistress Ford. I think my husband hath some special suspicion of Falstaff's being here; for I never saw him so gross in his jealousy till now. 180

Mistress Page. I will lay a plot to try that and we will yet have more tricks with Falstaff: his dissolute disease will scarce obey this medicine.

Mistress Ford. Shall we send that foolish carrion, Mistress Quickly, to him, and excuse his throwing into the water, and give him another hope, to betray him to another punishment?

Mistress Page. We will do it: let him be sent for tomorrow, eight o'clock, to have amends.

The seekers return down the stairs

Ford. I cannot find him: may be the knave bragged 190 of that he could not compass.

Mistress Page. Heard you that?

Mistress Ford. You use me well, Master Ford, do you?

Ford. Ay, I do so.

Mistress Ford. Heaven make you better than your thoughts.

Ford. Amen.

Mistress Page. You do yourself mighty wrong, Master Ford.

Ford. Ay, ay: I must bear it. 200

Evans. If there be any pody in the house, and in the chambers, and in the coffers, and in the presses...heaven forgive my sins at the day of judgement!

Caius. By gar, nor I too: there is no bodies.

Page. Fie, fie, Master Ford! are you not ashamed?

What spirit, what devil suggests this imagination? I would not ha' your distemper in this kind, for the wealth of Windsor Castle.

Ford. 'Tis my fault, Master Page—I suffer for it.

210 *Evans.* You suffer for a pad conscience: your wife is as honest a 'omans, as I will desires among five thousand, and five hundred too.

Caius. By gar, I see 'tis an honest woman.

Ford. Well, I promised you a dinner...Come, come, walk in the Park. I pray you, pardon me: I will hereafter make known to you why I have done this....Come, wife; come, Mistress Page—I pray you pardon me....[*takes their hands*] Pray heartily, pardon me.

[*Mistress Ford and Mistress Page go to prepare dinner*

Page [*to the others*]. Let's go in, gentlemen—but, trust 220 me, we'll mock him...I do invite you to-morrow morning to my house to breakfast: after, we'll a-birding together—I have a fine hawk for the bush....Shall it be so?

Ford. Any thing.

Evans. If there is one, I shall make two in the company.

Caius. If there be one or two, I shall mak-a the turd.

Ford. Pray you go, Master Page.

[*Ford and Page go forth to the Park*

Evans. I pray you now, remembrance to-morrow on the lousy knave, mine host.

Caius. Dat is good, by gar—vit all my heart.

230 *Evans.* A lousy knave, to have his gibes and his mockeries.

[*they follow Ford and Page*

[3. 4.] *Before the house of Master Page*

FENTON and ANNE seated, under the trees

Fenton. I see I cannot get thy father's love,
Therefore no more turn me to him, sweet Nan.

Anne. Alas, how then?

Fenton. Why, thou must be thyself....
He doth object I am too great of birth,
And that, my state being galled with my expense,
I seek to heal it only by his wealth....
Besides these, other bars he lays before me—
My riots past, my wild societies—
And tells me 'tis a thing impossible
I should love thee but as a property... 10
Anne. May be he tells you true.
Fenton. No, heaven so speed me in my time to come!
Albeit I will confess thy father's wealth
Was the first motive that I wooed thee, Anne:
Yet, wooing thee, I found thee of more value
Than stamps in gold or sums in sealéd bags:
And 'tis the very riches of thyself
That now I aim at.
Anne. Gentle Master Fenton,
Yet seek my father's love—still seek it, sir.
If opportunity and humblest suit 20
Cannot attain it, why then hark you hither!

The house-door opens suddenly; SHALLOW and SLENDER come forth with Mistress QUICKLY

Shallow. Break their talk, Mistress Quickly. My kinsman shall speak for himself. [*she draws near the lovers*
Slender [*pale*]. I'll make a shaft or a bolt on't. 'Slid, 'tis but venturing.
Shallow. Be not dismayed.
Slender. No, she shall not dismay me: I care not for that—but that I am afeard.
Quickly [*to Anne*]. Hark ye, Master Slender would speak a word with you. 30
Anne. I come to him....[*to Fenton*] This is my father's choice:

O, what a world of vile ill-favoured faults
Looks handsome in three hundred pounds a-year!

Quickly [*steps between them*]. And how does good Master Fenton? Pray you, a word with you. [*Anne moves away*

Shallow. She's coming; to her, coz...O boy, thou hadst a father!

Slender. I had a father, Mistress Anne. My uncle can tell you good jests of him: pray you, uncle, tell Mistress
40 Anne the jest, how my father stole two geese out of a pen, good uncle.

Shallow. Mistress Anne, my cousin loves you.

Slender. Ay, that I do—as well as I love any woman in Gloucestershire.

Shallow. He will maintain you like a gentlewoman.

Slender. Ay, that I will, come cut and long-tail—under the degree of a squire.

Shallow. He will make you a hundred and fifty pounds jointure.

50 *Anne*. Good Master Shallow, let him woo for himself.

Shallow. Marry, I thank you for it: I thank you for that good comfort...She calls you, coz. I'll leave you.

[*he stands aside*

Anne. Now, Master Slender.

Slender [*plucking at his beard*]. Now, good Mistress Anne.

Anne. What is your will?

Slender. My will! od's heartlings, that's a pretty jest, indeed. I ne'er made my will yet, I thank heaven! I am not such a sickly creature, I give heaven praise.

60 *Anne*. I mean, Master Slender, what would you with me?

Slender [*casting down his eyes*]. Truly, for mine own part, I would little or nothing with you...Your father and my uncle hath made motions: if it be my luck, so; if not, happy man be his dole! They can tell you how things go, better than I can: you may ask your father; here he comes.

PAGE and Mistress PAGE come up, returning from Master Ford's house

Page. Now, Master Slender; love him, daughter Anne....
Why, how now! what does Master Fenton here?
You wrong me, sir, thus still to haunt my house.... 70
I told you, sir, my daughter is disposed of.

Fenton. Nay, Master Page, be not impatient.

Mistress Page. Good Master Fenton, come not to my child.

Page. She is no match for you.

Fenton. Sir, will you hear me?

Page. No, good Master Fenton....
Come, Master Shallow; come, son Slender, in...
Knowing my mind, you wrong me, Master Fenton.

[*Page, Shallow and Slender enter the house*

Quickly. Speak to Mistress Page.

Fenton. Good Mistress Page, for that I love your daughter
In such a righteous fashion as I do, 80
Perforce, against all checks, rebukes and manners,
I must advance the colours of my love,
And not retire....Let me have your good will.

Anne. Good mother, do not marry me to yond fool.

Mistress Page. I mean it not. I seek you a better husband.

Quickly. That's my master, master doctor.

Anne. Alas, I had rather be set quick i'th'earth,
And bowled to death with turnips.

Mistress Page. Come, trouble not yourself good Master Fenton,
I will not be your friend nor enemy. 90

My daughter will I question how she loves you,
And as I find her, so am I affected:
Till then, farewell, sir. She must needs go in—
Her father will be angry.

Mistress Page goes in; Anne follows, turning at the door

Fenton. Farewell, gentle mistress: farewell, Nan.

[*the door closes*

Quickly. This is my doing now: 'Nay,' said I, 'will you cast away your child on a fool, and a physician? Look on Master Fenton.' This is my doing.

Fenton. I thank thee; and I pray thee, once to-night
100 Give my sweet Nan this ring...There's for thy pains.

He thrusts money in her hand and departs

Quickly. Now heaven send thee good fortune! A kind heart he hath: a woman would run through fire and water for such a kind heart....[*pockets the coin*] But yet, I would my master had Mistress Anne; or I would Master Slender had her; or, in sooth, I would Master Fenton had her: I will do what I can for them all three—for so I have promised, and I'll be as good as my word, but speciously for Master Fenton....Well, I must of another errand to Sir John Falstaff from my two mistresses:
110 what a beast am I to slack it! [*she hurries away*

[3. 5.] *The room in the Garter Inn: early morning*
FALSTAFF descends from his chamber

Falstaff [*calling*]. Bardolph, I say!

Bardolph [*runs in*]. Here, sir.

Falstaff. Go fetch me a quart of sack—put a toast in't....[*Bardolph goes; Falstaff sits*] Have I lived to be carried in a basket, like a barrow of butcher's offal, and to be thrown in the Thames? Well, if I be served such another trick, I'll have my brains ta'en out, and buttered, and give them to a dog for a new-year's gift....The rogues slighted me into the river with as little remorse as they would have drowned a blind bitch's puppies, 10 fifteen i'th' litter: and you may know by my size, that I have a kind of alacrity in sinking; if the bottom were as deep as hell, I should down....I had been drowned, but that the shore was shelvy and shallow...a death that I abhor; for the water swells a man, and what a thing should I have been, when I had been swelled! I should have been a mountain of mummy.

BARDOLPH returns with two cups of sack

Bardolph. Here's Mistress Quickly, sir, to speak with you. [*he sets the cups down*

Falstaff [*takes one*]. Come, let me pour in some sack to 20 the Thames water; for my belly's as cold as if I had swallowed snowballs for pills to cool the reins....[*he drains the cup*] Call her in.

Bardolph [*opening the door*]. Come in, woman.

Mistress QUICKLY enters and curtsies

Quickly. By your leave...I cry you mercy! Give your worship good-morrow.

Falstaff [*empties the second cup*]. Take away these chalices...Go brew me a pottle of sack finely.

Bardolph [*takes up the empty cups*]. With eggs, sir?

Falstaff. Simple of itself; I'll no pullet-sperm in my 30 brewage....[*Bardolph leaves*] How now!

Quickly. Marry, sir, I come to your worship from Mistress Ford.

Falstaff. Mistress Ford! I have had ford enough: I was thrown into the ford; I have my belly full of ford.

Quickly. Alas the day! good heart, that was not her fault: she does so take on with her men; they mistook their erection.

Falstaff. So did I mine, to build upon a foolish woman's
40 promise.

Quickly. Well, she laments, sir, for it, that it would yearn your heart to see it...Her husband goes this morning a-birding; she desires you once more to come to her, between eight and nine: I must carry her word quickly. She'll make you amends, I warrant you.

Falstaff. Well, I will visit her. Tell her so; and bid her think what a man is: let her consider his frailty, and then judge of my merit.

Quickly. I will tell her.

50 *Falstaff.* Do so....Between nine and ten, sayst thou?

Quickly. Eight and nine, sir.

Falstaff. Well, be gone: I will not miss her.

Quickly. Peace be with you, sir! [*she goes*

Falstaff. I marvel I hear not of Master Brook; he sent me word to stay within: I like his money well....O, here he comes.

FORD *enters, disguised as* BROOK

Ford. Bless you, sir!

Falstaff. Now, Master Brook—you come to know what hath passed between me and Ford's wife?

60 *Ford.* That, indeed, Sir John, is my business.

Falstaff. Master Brook, I will not lie to you. I was at her house the hour she appointed me—

Ford. And sped you, sir?

Falstaff. Very ill-favouredly, Master Brook.

Ford. How so, sir? Did she change her determination?

Falstaff. No, Master Brook—but the peaking cornuto her husband, Master Brook, dwelling in a continual 'larum of jealousy, comes me in the instant of our encounter, after we had embraced, kissed, protested, and, as it were,
70 spoke the prologue of our comedy; and at his heels a

rabble of his companions, thither provoked and instigated by his distemper, and, forsooth, to search his house for his wife's love.

Ford. What! while you were there?

Falstaff. While I was there.

Ford. And did he search for you, and could not find you?

Falstaff. You shall hear....As good luck would have it, comes in one Mistress Page, gives intelligence of Ford's approach...and, in her invention and Ford's wife's distraction, they conveyed me into a buck-basket. 80

Ford. A buck-basket!

Falstaff. [By the Lord,] a buck-basket: rammed me in with foul shirts and smocks, socks, foul stockings, greasy napkins—that, Master Brook, there was the rankest compound of villainous smell, that ever offended nostril.

Ford. And how long lay you there?

Falstaff. Nay, you shall hear, Master Brook, what I have suffered to bring this woman to evil for your good...Being thus crammed in the basket, a couple of Ford's knaves, 90 his hinds, were called forth by their mistress, to carry me in the name of foul clothes to Datchet-lane: they took me on their shoulders; met the jealous knave their master in the door; who asked them once or twice what they had in their basket! I quaked for fear, lest the lunatic knave would have searched it; but fate, ordaining he should be a cuckold, held his hand...Well, on went he for a search, and away went I for foul clothes: but mark the sequel, Master Brook. I suffered the pangs of three several deaths: first, an intolerable fright, to be detected with a jealous 100 rotten bell-wether; next, to be compassed, like a good bilbo, in the circumference of a peck, hilt to point, heel to head....and then, to be stopped in, like a strong distillation, with stinking clothes that fretted in their own

grease...think of that—a man of my kidney; think of that—that am as subject to heat, as butter; a man of continual dissolution and thaw; it was a miracle to 'scape suffocation....And in the height of this bath, when I was more than half stewed in grease, like a Dutch dish, to be
110 thrown into the Thames, and cooled, glowing-hot (in that surge!) like a horse-shoe; think of that—hissing hot; think of that, Master Brook!

Ford. In good sadness, sir, I am sorry that for my sake you have suffered all this....My suit then is desperate: you'll undertake her no more?

Falstaff. Master Brook...I will be thrown into Etna, as I have been into Thames, ere I will leave her thus...Her husband is this morning gone a-birding: I have received from her another embassy of meeting: 'twixt eight and
120 nine is the hour, Master Brook.

Ford. 'Tis past eight already, sir.

Falstaff. Is it? I will then address me to my appointment...Come to me at your convenient leisure, and you shall know how I speed: and the conclusion shall be crowned with your enjoying her...Adieu...You shall have her, Master Brook. Master Brook, you shall cuckold Ford. [*he goes out*

Ford. Hum...ha! is this a vision? is this a dream? do I sleep? Master Ford awake, awake Master Ford! there's a hole made in your best coat, Master Ford...This 'tis to
130 be married; this 'tis to have linen and buck-baskets... Well, I will proclaim myself what I am: I will now take the lecher: he is at my house: he cannot 'scape me: 'tis impossible he should: he cannot creep into a halfpenny purse, nor into a pepper-box...But, lest the devil that guides him should aid him, I will search impossible places ...Though what I am I cannot avoid, yet to be what I would not shall not make me tame: if I have horns to

make one mad, let the proverb go with me—I'll be horn-mad. [*he rushes out*

[4. 1.] *The street before the house of Master Page*

Mistress PAGE *comes forth with Mistress* QUICKLY, *and* WILLIAM

Mistress Page. Is he at Master Ford's already, think'st thou?

Quickly. Sure, he is by this; or will be presently; but truly he is very courageous mad, about his throwing into the water....Mistress Ford desires you to come suddenly.

Mistress Page. I'll be with her by and by: I'll but bring my young man here to school...Look where his master comes; 'tis a playing-day, I see...

Sir HUGH EVANS *approaches*

How now, Sir Hugh! no school to-day?

Evans. No: Master Slender is let the boys leave to play. 10

Quickly. Blessing of his heart!

Mistress Page. Sir Hugh, my husband says my son profits nothing in the world at his book: I pray you, ask him some questions in his accidence.

Evans. Come hither, William; hold up your head; come.

Mistress Page. Come on, sirrah; hold up your head; answer your master, be not afraid.

Evans. William, how many numbers is in nouns?

William. Two. 20

Quickly. Truly, I thought there had been one number more; because they say, 'Od's nouns.'

Evans. Peace your tattlings! What is 'fair,' William?

William. Pulcher.

Quickly. Polecats! there are fairer things than polecats, sure.

Evans. You are a very simplicity 'oman: I pray you, peace....What is 'lapis,' William?

William. A stone.

30 *Evans.* And what is 'a stone,' William?

William. A pebble.

Evans. No; it is 'lapis': I pray you remember in your prain.

William. Lapis.

Evans. That is a good William...What is he, William, that does lend articles?

William. Articles are borrowed of the pronoun; and be thus declined, Singulariter, nominativo, hic, hæc, hoc.

Evans. Nominativo, hig, hag, hog: pray you, mark: genitivo, hujus...Well: what is your accusative case?

40 *William.* Accusativo, hinc.

Evans. I pray you, have your remembrance, child—accusativo, hung, hang, hog.

Quickly. 'Hang-hog' is Latin for bacon, I warrant you.

Evans. Leave your prabbles, 'oman....What is the focative case, William?

William [*scratches his head*]. O! vocativo—O.

Evans. Remember, William—focative is caret.

Quickly. And that's a good root.

Evans. 'Oman, forbear.

50 *Mistress Page.* Peace.

Evans. What is your genitive case plural, William?

William. Genitive case?

Evans. Ay.

William. Genitive—horum, harum, horum.

Quickly. Vengeance of Jenny's case! fie on her! never name her, child, if she be a whore.

Evans. For shame, 'oman.

Quickly. You do ill to teach the child such words: he teaches him to hick and to hack—which they'll do fast

60 enough of themselves, and to call 'horum'; fie upon you!

Evans. 'Oman, art thou lunatics? hast thou no understandings for thy cases, and the numbers of the genders? Thou art as foolish Christian creatures as I would desires.

Mistress Page [*to Mistress Quickly*]. Prithee hold thy peace.

Evans. Show me now, William, some declensions of your pronouns.

William. Forsooth, I have forgot.

Evans. It is qui, quæ, quod; if you forget your qui's, your quæ's, and your quod's, you must be preeches... 70 Go your ways and play, go.

Mistress Page. He is a better scholar than I thought he was.

Evans. He is a good sprag memory...Farewell, Mistress Page. [*he pursues his way*

Mistress Page. Adieu, good Sir Hugh...Get you home, boy. Come, we stay too long.

[*she goes off with Mistress Quickly*

[4. 2.] *The hall in Master Ford's house; the buck-basket in a corner*

FALSTAFF and Mistress FORD, seated

Falstaff. Mistress Ford, your sorrow hath eaten up my sufferance; I see you are obsequious in your love, and I profess requital to a hair's breadth, not only, Mistress Ford, in the simple office of love, but in all the accoutrement, complement, and ceremony of it...But are you sure of your husband now?

Mistress Ford. He's a-birding, sweet Sir John.

Mistress Page [*calling without*]. What ho, gossip Ford! what ho!

Mistress Ford [*opening a door*]. Step into th' chamber, 10 Sir John. [*Falstaff goes forth, leaving the door ajar*

Mistress PAGE *enters*

Mistress Page. How now, sweetheart! who's at home besides yourself?

Mistress Ford. Why, none but mine own people.

Mistress Page. Indeed?

Mistress Ford. No, certainly...[*whispers*] Speak louder.

Mistress Page. Truly, I am so glad you have nobody here.

Mistress Ford. Why?

Mistress Page. Why, woman, your husband is in his old
20 †lunes again: he so takes on yonder with my husband; so rails against all married mankind; so curses all Eve's daughters, of what complexion soever; and so buffets himself on the forehead, crying, 'Peer out, peer out!' that any madness I ever yet beheld seemed but tameness, civility, and patience, to this his distemper he is in now... I am glad the fat knight is not here.

Mistress Ford. Why, does he talk of him?

Mistress Page. Of none but him—and swears he was carried out the last time he searched for him in a basket;
30 protests to my husband he is now here; and hath drawn him and the rest of their company from their sport, to make another experiment of his suspicion...But I am glad the knight is not here; now he shall see his own foolery.

Mistress Ford. How near is he, Mistress Page?

Mistress Page. Hard by, at street end; he will be here anon.

Mistress Ford. I am undone!—the knight is here.

Mistress Page. Why, then you are utterly shamed, and
40 he's but a dead man....What a woman are you! Away with him, away with him: better shame than murder!

FALSTAFF *peers forth from the chamber*

Mistress Ford. Which way should he go? how should I bestow him? Shall I put him into the basket again?

Falstaff [*rushes forward*]. No, I'll come no more i'th' basket...May I not go out, ere he come?

Mistress Page. Alas: three of Master Ford's brothers watch the door with pistols, that none shall issue out: otherwise you might slip away ere he came...But what make you here?

Falstaff. What shall I do?—I'll creep up into the chimney. 50

†*Mistress Page.* There they always use to discharge their birding-pieces...Creep into the kiln-hole.

Falstaff. Where is it?

Mistress Ford. He will seek there on my word...Neither press, coffer, chest, trunk, well, vault, but he hath an abstract for the remembrance of such places, and goes to them by his note...There is no hiding you in the house.

Falstaff [*at bay*]. I'll go out then.

†*Mistress Page.* If you go out in your own semblance, 60 you die, Sir John—unless you go out disguised.

Mistress Ford. How might we disguise him?

Mistress Page. Alas the day, I know not. There is no woman's gown big enough for him; otherwise, he might put on a hat, a muffler, and a kerchief, and so escape.

Falstaff. Good hearts, devise something: any extremity, rather than a mischief.

Mistress Ford. My maid's aunt, the fat woman of Brainford, has a gown above. 70

Mistress Page. On my word, it will serve him; she's as big as he is: and there's her thrummed hat, and her muffler too...Run up, Sir John.

Mistress Ford. Go, go, sweet Sir John...Mistress Page and I will look some linen for your head.

Mistress Page. Quick, quick! we'll come dress you straight: put on the gown the while.

[*Falstaff posts up the stairs*

Mistress Ford. I would my husband would meet him in this shape: he cannot abide the old woman of Brain-
80 ford; he swears she's a witch, forbade her my house, and hath threatened to beat her.

Mistress Page. Heaven guide him to thy husband's cudgel: and the devil guide his cudgel afterwards!

Mistress Ford. But is my husband coming?

Mistress Page. Ay, in good sadness, is he—and talks of the basket too, howsoever he hath had intelligence.

Mistress Ford. We'll try that; for I'll appoint my men to carry the basket again, to meet him at the door with it, as they did last time.

90 *Mistress Page.* Nay, but he'll be here presently: let's go dress him like the witch of Brainford.

Mistress Ford. I'll first direct my men what they shall do with the basket...Go up, I'll bring linen for him straight.

Mistress Page. Hang him, dishonest varlet! we cannot misuse him enough...

[*Mistress Ford goes out; Mistress Page mounts the stairs*

We'll leave a proof, by that which we will do,
Wives may be merry, and yet honest too:
We do not act that often jest and laugh—
100 'Tis old but true, 'Still swine eats all the draff.'

Mistress FORD *returns with the two servants*

Mistress Ford. Go, sirs, take the basket again on your shoulders: your master is hard at door: if he bid you set it down, obey him...quickly, dispatch.

[*she takes linen from a cupboard and goes upstairs*

First Servant. Come, come, take it up.

Second Servant. Pray heaven it be not full of knight again.

First Servant. I hope not. I had as lief bear so much lead. [*they lift the basket*

The door opens; FORD, PAGE, SHALLOW, CAIUS, *and* Sir HUGH EVANS *enter from the street*

Ford. Ay, but if it prove true, Master Page, have you any way then to unfool me again? [*the basket catches* 110 *his eye*]....Set down the basket, villain...Somebody call my wife...Youth in a basket...O, you pandarly rascals! there's a knot...a ging, a pack, a conspiracy against me...Now shall the devil be shamed [*chokes*]....What! wife, I say...Come, come forth...Behold what honest clothes you send forth to bleaching!

Page. Why, this passes, Master Ford! you are not to go loose any longer—you must be pinioned.

Evans. Why, this is lunatics! this is mad, as a mad dog! 120

Shallow. Indeed, Master Ford, this is not well, indeed.

Ford. So say I too, sir. [*Mistress Ford appears in the gallery*] Come hither, Mistress Ford! [*pointing, as she descends*] Mistress Ford, the honest woman, the modest wife, the virtuous creature, that hath the jealous fool to her husband...[*she confronts him*] I suspect without cause, mistress, do I?

Mistress Ford [*calm*]. Heaven be my witness you do, if you suspect me in any dishonesty.

Ford. Well said, brazen-face, hold it out...Come forth, 130 sirrah. [*plucking forth the clothes in a fury*

Page. This passes!

Mistress Ford. Are you not ashamed? let the clothes alone.

Ford. I shall find you anon.

Evans. 'Tis unreasonable! Will you take up your wife's clothes? [*to the others*] Come, away!

Ford [*to the servants*]. Empty the basket, I say.

Mistress Ford. Why, man, why?

140 *Ford.* Master Page, as I am a man, there was one conveyed out of my house yesterday in this basket: why may not he be there again? In my house I am sure he is: my intelligence is true, my jealousy is reasonable, pluck me out all the linen! [*Page assists him*

Mistress Ford. If you find a man there, he shall die a flea's death.

Page. Here's no man. [*he overturns the empty basket*

Shallow. By my fidelity, this is not well, Master Ford: this wrongs you.

150 *Evans.* Master Ford, you must pray, and not follow the imaginations of your own heart: this is jealousies.

Ford. Well, he's not here I seek for.

Page. No, nor nowhere else but in your brain.

Ford. Help to search my house this one time: if I find not what I seek, show no colour for my extremity...let me for ever be your table-sport...let them say of me, 'As jealous as Ford, that searched a hollow walnut for his wife's leman'....Satisfy me once more, once more search with me.

160 *Mistress Ford.* What ho, Mistress Page! come you and the old woman down: my husband will come into the chamber.

Ford. Old woman! What old woman's that?

Mistress Ford. Why, it is my maid's aunt of Brainford.

Ford. A witch, a quean, an old cozening quean! Have I not forbid her my house? She comes of errands, does she? We are simple men, we do not know what's brought to pass under the profession of fortune-telling....She works

by charms, by spells, by th' figure, and such daubery as 170
this is, beyond our element: we know nothing....[*he takes down his cudgel from the wall*] Come down, you witch, you hag you, come down, I say.

Mistress Ford. Nay, good, sweet husband—good gentlemen, let him not strike the old woman.

FALSTAFF descends in women's clothes, led by Mistress PAGE; he hesitates near the foot of the stairs

Mistress Page. Come, Mother Prat, come, give me your hand.

Ford. I'll prat her...[*Falstaff runs; Ford cudgels*] Out of my door, you witch, you rag, you baggage, you polecat, you ronyon! out! out! I'll conjure you, I'll fortune-tell 180
you. [*Falstaff escapes into the street*

Mistress Page. Are you not ashamed? I think, you have killed the poor woman.

Mistress Ford. Nay, he will do it. 'Tis a goodly credit for you.

Ford. Hang her, witch! [*he mounts the stairs*

Evans. By yea and no, I think the 'oman is a witch indeed: I like not when a 'oman has a great peard; I spy a great peard under his muffler.

Ford [*from the gallery*]. Will you follow, gentlemen? I 190
beseech you, follow: see but the issue of my jealousy: if I cry out thus upon no trail, never trust me when I open again.

Page. Let's obey his humour a little further...Come, gentlemen. [*they follow*

Mistress Page. Trust me, he beat him most pitifully.

Mistress Ford. Nay, by th' mass, that he did not: he beat him most unpitifully methought.

Mistress Page. I'll have the cudgel hallowed and hung o'er the altar—it hath done meritorious service. 200

Mistress Ford. What think you? May we, with the warrant of womanhood and the witness of a good conscience, pursue him with any further revenge?

Mistress Page. The spirit of wantonness is, sure, scared out of him. If the devil have him not in fee-simple, with fine and recovery, he will never, I think, in the way of waste, attempt us again.

Mistress Ford. Shall we tell our husbands how we have served him?

210 *Mistress Page.* Yes, by all means; if it be but to scrape the figures out of your husband's brains...If they can find in their hearts the poor unvirtuous fat knight shall be any further afflicted, we two will still be the ministers.

Mistress Ford. I'll warrant they'll have him publicly shamed—and methinks there would be no period to the jest, should he not be publicly shamed.

Mistress Page. Come, to the forge with it! then shape it: I would not have things cool.

[*they go up together, talking*

[4. 3.] *The room in the Garter Inn*

HOST and BARDOLPH enter

Bardolph. Sir, the Germans desire to have three of your horses: the duke himself will be to-morrow at court, and they are going to meet him.

Host. What duke should that be comes so secretly? I hear not of him in the court...Let me speak with the gentlemen—they speak English?

Bardolph. Ay, sir; I'll call them to you.

Host. They shall have my horses, but I'll make them pay: I'll sauce them. They have had my house a week at

10 command; I have turned away my other guests. They must come off. I'll sauce them, come. [*they go out*

[4. 4.] *The hall in Master Ford's house*

PAGE, FORD, Mistress PAGE, Mistress FORD, and Sir HUGH EVANS, holding lively conversation

Evans. 'Tis one of the pest discretions of a 'oman as ever I did look upon.

Page. And did he send you both these letters at an instant?

Mistress Page. Within a quarter of an hour.

Ford [*kneeling*]. Pardon me, wife. Henceforth do what thou wilt:
I rather will suspect the sun with cold
Than thee with wantonness: now doth thy honour stand,
In him that was of late an heretic,
As firm as faith.

Page. 'Tis well, 'tis well—no more: 10
Be not as éxtreme in submission,
As in offence.
But let our plot go forward: let our wives
Yet once again, to make us public sport,
Appoint a meeting with this old fat fellow,
Where we may take him, and disgrace him for it.

Ford. There is no better way than that they spoke of.

Page. How? to send him word they'll meet him in the Park at midnight? fie, fie! he'll never come.

Evans. You say he has been thrown in the rivers, and 20 has been grievously peaten, as an old 'oman: methinks there should be terrors in him, that he should not come: methinks his flesh is punished, he shall have no desires.

Page. So think I too.

Mistress Ford. Devise but how you'll use him, when he comes,
And let us two devise to bring him thither.

Mistress Page. There is an old tale goes, that Herne the hunter,
Sometime a keeper here in Windsor forest,
30 Doth all the winter-time, at still midnight,
Walk round about an oak, with great ragg'd horns—
And there he blasts the tree, and takes the cattle,
And makes milch-kine yield blood, and shakes a chain
In a most hideous and dreadful manner....
You have heard of such a spirit, and well you know
The superstitious idle-headed eld
Received, and did deliver to our age,
This tale of Herne the hunter for a truth.
Page. Why, yet there want not many that do fear
40 In deep of night to walk by this Herne's oak:
But what of this?
Mistress Ford. Marry, this is our device—
That Falstaff at that oak shall meet with us,
[Disguised like Herne, with huge horns on his head.]
Page. Well, let it not be doubted but he'll come,
And in this shape. When you have brought him thither
What shall be done with him? what is your plot?
Mistress Page. That likewise have we thought upon, and thus:
Nan Page my daughter and my little son
And three or four more of their growth we'll dress
50 Like urchins, ouphs, and fairies, green and white,
With rounds of waxen tapers on their heads,
And rattles in their hands; upon a sudden,
As Falstaff, she, and I, are newly met,
Let them from forth a saw-pit rush at once
With some diffuséd song: upon their sight,
We two in great amazédness will fly:
Then let them all encircle him about,
And, fairy-like, to pinch the unclean knight;

And ask him why, that hour of fairy revel,
In their so sacred paths he dares to tread 60
In shape profane.
Mistress Ford. And till he tell the truth,
Let the supposéd fairies pinch him sound,
And burn him with their tapers.
Mistress Page. The truth being known,
We'll all present ourselves; dis-horn the spirit,
And mock him home to Windsor.
Ford. The children must
Be practised well to this, or they'll ne'er do't.
Evans. I will teach the children their behaviours: and
I will be like a jack-an-apes also, to burn the knight with
my taber.
Ford. That will be excellent. I'll go buy them vizards. 70
Mistress Page. My Nan shall be the queen of all
the fairies,
Finely attiréd in a robe of white.
Page. That silk will I go buy—[*aside*] and in that time
Shall Master Slender steal my Nan away,
And marry her at Eton...Go, send to Falstaff straight.
Ford [*to Page*]. Nay, I'll to him again in name of Brook:
He'll tell me all his purpose: sure, he'll come.
Mistress Page. Fear not you that...Go, get us properties,
And tricking for our fairies.
Evans. Let us about it: it is admirable pleasures and 80
fery honest knaveries. [*Page, Ford, and Evans depart*
Mistress Page. Go, Mistress Ford,
Send Quickly to Sir John, to know his mind...
[*Mistress Ford goes*
I'll to the doctor—he hath my good will,
And none but he, to marry with Nan Page...
That Slender, though well landed, is an idiot;
And he my husband best of all affects:

The doctor is well moneyed, and his friends
Potent at court: he, none but he, shall have her,
90 Though twenty thousand worthier come to crave her.
[*she goes*

[4. 5.] *The room in the Garter Inn*

SIMPLE stands waiting; HOST enters in haste

Host. What wouldst thou have, boor? what, thick-skin? speak, breathe, discuss; brief, short, quick, snap.

Simple. Marry, sir, I come to speak with Sir John Falstaff from Master Slender.

Host [*points to the gallery*]. There's his chamber, his house, his castle, his standing-bed, and truckle-bed; 'tis painted about with the story of the Prodigal, fresh and new: go, knock and call: he'll speak like an Anthropophaginian unto thee: knock, I say.

10 *Simple.* There's an old woman, a fat woman, gone up into his chamber: I'll be so bold as stay, sir, till she come down: I come to speak with her, indeed.

Host. Ha! a fat woman! the knight may be robbed: I'll call....Bully knight! bully Sir John! speak from thy lungs military: art thou there? it is thine host, thine Ephesian, calls.

Falstaff [*opens the door of his chamber*]. How now, mine host?

Host. Here's a Bohemian-Tartar tarries the coming
20 down of thy fat woman...Let her descend, bully, let her descend: my chambers are honourable: fie! privacy? fie!

FALSTAFF descends

Falstaff. There was, mine host, an old fat woman even now with me—but she's gone.

Simple. Pray you, sir, was't not the wise woman of Brainford?

Falstaff. Ay, marry, was it, mussel-shell—what would you with her?

Simple. My master, sir, Master Slender, sent to her, seeing her go thorough the streets, to know, sir, whether one Nym, sir, that beguiled him of a chain, had the chain, or no. 30

Falstaff. I spake with the old woman about it.

Simple. And what says she, I pray, sir?

Falstaff. Marry, she says that the very same man that beguiled Master Slender of his chain cozened him of it.

Simple. I would I could have spoken with the woman herself. I had other things to have spoken with her too, from him.

Falstaff. What are they? let us know.

Host. Ay...come...quick!

Simple. I may not conceal them, sir. 40

Host [*threatening him*]. Conceal them, or thou diest.

Simple. Why, sir, they were nothing but about Mistress Anne Page—to know if it were my master's fortune to have her, or no.

Falstaff. 'Tis, 'tis his fortune.

Simple. What, sir?

Falstaff. To have her, or no...Go; say the woman told me so.

Simple. May I be so bold to say so, sir?

Falstaff. Ay, Sir †Tyke; who more bold? 50

Simple. I thank your worship: I shall make my master glad with these tidings. [*he goes out*

Host. Thou art clerkly! thou art clerkly, Sir John. Was there a wise woman with thee?

Falstaff. Ay, that there was, mine host—one that hath taught me more wit than ever I learned before in my life: and I paid nothing for it neither, but was paid for my learning.

BARDOLPH enters, mired and breathless

Bardolph. Out, alas, sir! cozenage...mere cozenage!

60 *Host.* Where be my horses? speak well of them, varletto.

Bardolph. Run away with the cozeners...for so soon as I came beyond Eton, they threw me off, from behind one of them, in a slough of mire...and set spurs, and away... like three German devils...three Doctor Faustuses.

Host. They are gone but to meet the duke, villain. Do not say, they be fled; Germans are honest men.

Sir HUGH EVANS opens the door and looks in

Evans. Where is mine host?

Host. What is the matter, sir?

Evans. Have a care of your entertainments: there is a

70 friend of mine come to town, tells me there is three cozen-germans that has cozened all the hosts of Readins, of Maidenhead, of Colebrook, of horses and money...I tell you for good will, look you! you are wise, and full of gibes and vlouting-stogs...and 'tis not convenient you should be cozened! Fare you well. [*he claps the door to*

Doctor CAIUS opens the door and looks in

Caius. Vere is mine host de Jarteer?

Host. Here, master doctor, in perplexity and doubtful dilemma.

Caius. I cannot tell vat is dat: but it is tell-a me dat

80 you make grand preparation for a duke de Jarmany: by my trot, dere is no duke dat de court is know to come: I tell you for good vill: adieu. [*he claps the door to*

Host. Hue and cry, villain! go...Assist me, knight. I am undone...Fly, run...hue and cry, villain! I am undone!

[*he runs forth with Bardolph after*

Falstaff. I would all the world might be cozened, for I have been cozened and beaten too...If it should come to the ear of the court, how I have been transformed... and how my transformation hath been washed and cudgelled, they would melt me out of my fat, drop by drop, and liquor fishermen's boots with me: I warrant 90 they would whip me with their fine wits till I were as crest-fallen as a dried pear...I never prospered since I forswore myself at primero: well, if my wind were but long enough [to say my prayers], I would repent...

Mistress QUICKLY enters

Now! whence come you?

Quickly. From the two parties, forsooth.

Falstaff. The devil take one party, and his dam the other! and so they shall be both bestowed...I have suffered more for their sakes—more than the villainous inconstancy of man's disposition is able to bear. 100

Quickly. And have not they suffered? Yes, I warrant; speciously one of them; Mistress Ford, good heart! is beaten black and blue, that you cannot see a white spot about her.

Falstaff. What, tell'st thou me of black and blue! I was beaten myself into all the colours of the rainbow: and I was like to be apprehended for the witch of Brainford. But that my admirable dexterity of wit, my counterfeiting the action of an old woman, delivered me, the knave constable had set me i'th' stocks, i'th' common 110 stocks, for a witch.

Quickly. Sir: let me speak with you in your chamber, you shall hear how things go, and I warrant to your content...Here is a letter will say somewhat...Good hearts, what ado here is to bring you together! Sure, one of you does not serve heaven well, that you are so crossed.

Falstaff. Come up into my chamber. [*they go up*

[4. 6.] *HOST returns, with FENTON*

Host. Master Fenton, talk not to me,
My mind is heavy: I will give over all.
Fenton. Yet hear me speak: assist me in my purpose,
And, as I am a gentleman, I'll give thee
A hundred pound in gold more than your loss.
Host. I will hear you, Master Fenton; and I will at the least keep your counsel.
Fenton. From time to time I have acquainted you
With the dear love I bear to fair Anne Page,
10 Who mutually hath answered my affection,
So far forth as herself might be her chooser,
Even to my wish; I have a letter from her
Of such contents as you will wonder at;
The mirth whereof so larded with my matter,
That neither, singly, can be manifested,
Without the show of both: fat Falstaff
Hath a great scene; the image of the jest
I'll show you here at large. Hark, good mine host...
[*he peruses the letter*
To-night at Herne's oak, just 'twixt twelve and one,
20 Must my sweet Nan present the Fairy-Queen...
The purpose why, is here...in which disguise,
While other jests are something rank on foot,
Her father hath commanded her to slip
Away with Slender, and with him at Eton
Immediately to marry: she hath consented...
Now, sir,
Her mother, ever strong against that match
And firm for Doctor Caius, hath appointed
That he shall likewise shuffle her away,
30 While other sports are tasking of their minds,

And at the deanery, where a priest attends,
Straight marry her: to this her mother's plot
She seemingly obedient likewise hath
Made promise to the doctor...Now, thus it rests—
Her father means she shall be all in white;
And in that habit, when Slender sees his time
To take her by the hand and bid her go,
She shall go with him: her mother hath intended—
The better to denote her to the doctor,
For they must all be masked and vizarded— 40
That quaint in green she shall be loose enrobed,
With ribands pendent, flaring 'bout her head;
And when the doctor spies his vantage ripe,
To pinch her by the hand, and, on that token,
The maid hath given consent to go with him.

Host. Which means she to deceive? father or mother?

Fenton. Both, my good host, to go along with me:
And here it rests—that you'll procure the vicar
To stay for me at church, 'twixt twelve and one,
And, in the lawful name of marrying, 50
To give our hearts united ceremony.

Host. Well, husband your device; I'll to the vicar.
Bring you the maid, you shall not lack a priest.

Fenton. So shall I evermore be bound to thee;
Besides, I'll make a present recompence. [*they go out*

[5. 1.] *FALSTAFF and Mistress QUICKLY come down from the chamber*

Falstaff. Prithee, no more prattling: go. I'll hold. This is the third time: I hope good luck lies in odd numbers...Away, go. They say there is divinity in odd numbers, either in nativity, chance, or death...Away!

Quickly. I'll provide you a chain, and I'll do what I can to get you a pair of horns.

Falstaff. Away, I say—time wears—hold up your head, and mince.... [*Mistress Quickly trips out; Ford enters*
How now, Master Brook! Master Brook, the matter will
10 be known to-night, or never....Be you in the Park about midnight, at Herne's oak, and you shall see wonders.

Ford. Went you not to her yesterday, sir, as you told me you had appointed?

Falstaff. I went to her, Master Brook, as you see, like a poor old man, but I came from her, Master Brook, like a poor old woman...That same knave Ford, her husband, hath the finest mad devil of jealousy in him, Master Brook, that ever governed frenzy....I will tell you he beat me grievously, in the shape of a woman: for in the
20 shape of man, Master Brook, I fear not Goliath with a weaver's beam, because I know also life is a shuttle. I am in haste—go along with me—I'll tell you all, Master Brook ...[*donning his cloak*] Since I plucked geese, played truant, and whipped top, I knew not what it was to be beaten, till lately....[*at the door*] Follow me. I'll tell you strange things of this knave Ford, on whom to-night I will be revenged, and I will deliver his wife into your hand.... [*goes out*] Follow. Strange things in hand, Master Brook! follow. [*Ford follows, smiling*

[5. 2.] *The outskirts of Windsor Park; night*

PAGE, SHALLOW, and SLENDER appear, with a lantern

Page. Come, come; we'll couch i'th' castle-ditch till we see the light of our fairies.... Remember, son Slender, my daughter.

Slender. Ay, forsooth—I have spoke with her, and we have a nay-word how to know one another....I come to her in white, and cry 'mum'; she cries 'budget,' and by that we know one another.

Shallow. That's good too: but what needs either your 'mum' or her 'budget'? the white will decipher her well enough....It hath struck ten o'clock. 10

Page. The night is dark—light and spirits will become it well...Heaven prosper our sport! No man means evil but the devil, and we shall know him by his horns....Let's away; follow me. [*they enter the Park*

[5. 3.] *Mistress* PAGE, *Mistress* FORD, *and Doctor* CAIUS *come up*

Mistress Page. Master doctor, my daughter is in green. When you see your time, take her by the hand, away with her to the deanery, and dispatch it quickly...Go before into the Park: we two must go together.

Caius. I know vat I have to do. Adieu. [*he goes on*

Mistress Page. Fare you well, sir....My husband will not rejoice so much at the abuse of Falstaff as he will chafe at the doctor's marrying my daughter: but 'tis no matter; better a little chiding than a great deal of heart-break.

Mistress Ford. Where is Nan now, and her troop of 10 fairies, and the Welsh †devil-hern?

Mistress Page. They are all couched in a pit hard by Herne's oak, with obscured lights; which at the very instant of Falstaff's and our meeting, they will at once display to the night.

Mistress Ford. That cannot choose but amaze him.

Mistress Page. If he be not amazed, he will be mocked; if he be amazed, he will every way be mocked.

Mistress Ford. We'll betray him finely.

Mistress Page. Against such lewdsters and their lechery
Those that betray them do no treachery. 20

Mistress Ford. The hour draws on...To the oak, to the oak! [*they enter the Park*

[5. 4.] *The Fairies approach, dancing, with masked lights: Sir* HUGH EVANS, *disguised as a Satyr in frieze and horns;* PISTOL *attired as Puck;* QUICKLY *in white as Fairy-Queen;* ANNE PAGE *with* WILLIAM, *and many other boys, in red, black, grey, green and white*

Evans. Trib, trib, fairies; come; and remember your parts: be pold, I pray you; follow me into the pit; and when I give the watch-'ords, do as I pid you...Come, come—trib, trib. [*they enter the Park*

[5. 5.] *Beneath a mighty oak in Windsor Park*

FALSTAFF *disguised as Herne the hunter, 'with a buck's head upon him'*

Falstaff. The Windsor bell hath struck twelve: the minute draws on...Now, the hot-blooded gods assist me! Remember, Jove, thou wast a bull for thy Europa—love set on thy horns....O powerful love, that, in some respects, makes a beast a man; in some other, a man a beast....You were also, Jupiter, a swan, for the love of Leda...O omnipotent love, how near the god drew to the complexion of a goose: a fault done first in the form of a beast—O Jove, a beastly fault!—and then another 10 fault in the semblance of a fowl—think on't, Jove, a foul fault! When gods have hot backs, what shall poor men do? For me, I am here a Windsor stag, and the fattest, I think, i'th' forest....Send me a cool rut-time, Jove, or who can blame me to piss my tallow? Who comes here? my doe?

Mistress FORD *comes from a thicket; Mistress* PAGE *following*

Mistress Ford. Sir John? art thou there—my deer? my male deer?

Falstaff. My doe with the black scut! Let the sky rain

potatoes; let it thunder to the tune of 'Green-sleeves,'
hail kissing-comfits, and snow eringoes; let there come 20
a tempest of provocation, I will shelter me here.

[*he embraces her*

Mistress Ford. Mistress Page is come with me, sweet-heart.

Falstaff. Divide me like a bribed-buck, each a haunch: I will keep my sides to myself, my shoulders for the fellow of this walk—and my horns I bequeath your husbands! Am I a woodman, ha? Speak I like Herne the hunter? Why, now is Cupid a child of conscience—he makes restitution....As I am a true spirit, welcome!

['*there is a noise of horns*'

Mistress Page. Alas! what noise? 30

Mistress Ford. Heaven forgive our sins!

Falstaff. What should this be?

Mistress Ford, Mistress Page. Away, away!

['*the two women run away*'

Falstaff. I think the devil will not have me damned,
Lest the oil that's in me should set hell on fire;
—he would never else cross me thus.

A sudden burst of light; the Fairies appear with crowns of fire and rattles in their hands, led by a Satyr holding a taper; they dance towards FALSTAFF, *singing*

Fairy-Queen. Fairies, black, grey, green, and white,
You moonshine revellers, and shades of night,
You orphan heirs of fixéd destiny,
Attend your office, and your quality.... 40
Crier Hobgoblin, make the fairy oyes.

Puck. Elves, list your names: silence, you airy toys....

[*they are still*

Cricket, to Windsor chimneys shalt thou leap;
Where fires thou find'st unraked and hearths unswept,

There pinch the maids as blue as bilberry.
Our radiant queen hates sluts and sluttery.
Falstaff. They are fairies! he that speaks to them shall die.
I'll wink and couch: no man their works must eye.
[*he lies upon his face at the foot of the oak*
Satyr. Where's Bead? Go you, and where you find a maid
50 That, ere she sleep, has thrice her prayers said,
Raise up the organs of her fantasy,
Sleep she as sound as careless infancy.
But those as sleep and think not on their sins,
Pinch them, arms, legs, backs, shoulders, sides, and shins.
Fairy-Queen. About, about...
Search Windsor Castle, elves, within and out....
Strew good luck, ouphs, on every sacred room,
That it may stand till the perpetual doom,
In state as wholesome as in state 'tis fit,
60 Worthy the owner, and the owner it....
The several chairs of order look you scour
With juice of balm, and every precious flower:
Each fair instalment, coat, and several crest,
With loyal blazon, evermore be blest!
And nightly, meadow-fairies, look you sing,
Like to the Garter's compass, in a ring.
Th'expressure that it bears, green let it be,
More fertile-fresh than all the field to see;
And, 'Honi soit qui mal y pense' write,
70 In emerald tufts, flowers purple, blue, and white—
Like sapphire, pearl, and rich embroidery,
Buckled below fair knighthood's bending knee:
Fairies use flowers for their charáctery....
Away, disperse! but till 'tis one o'clock,
Our dance of custom round about the oak
Of Herne the hunter, let us not forget.

Satyr. Pray you, lock hand in hand; yourselves in order set... [*the Fairies encircle the oak*
And twenty glow-worms shall our lanterns be,
To guide our measure round about the tree....
But stay—I smell a man of middle earth. 80
Falstaff. Heavens defend me from that Welsh fairy,
Lest he transform me to a piece of cheese!
Puck. Vile worm, thou wast o'er-looked even in thy birth.
Fairy-Queen. With trial-fire touch me his finger-end:
If he be chaste, the flame will back descend,
And turn him to no pain; but if he start,
It is the flesh of a corrupted heart.
Puck. A trial, come!
Satyr [*setting his light to the buck's horns*]. Come: will this wood take fire?
['*they put the tapers to his fingers, and he starts*'
Falstaff. Oh, oh, oh!
Fairy-Queen. Corrupt, corrupt, and tainted in desire! 90
About him, fairies, sing a scornful rhyme—
And, as you trip, still pinch him to your time.

The Fairies dance about him and sing:

Fie on sinful fantasy: fie on lust and luxury:
Lust is but a bloody fire, kindled with unchaste desire,
Fed in heart, whose flames aspire,
As thoughts do blow them, higher and higher.
Pinch him, fairies, mutually: pinch him for his villainy.
Pinch him, and burn him, and turn him about,
Till candles, and star-light, and moon-shine be out.

As they sing, they pinch FALSTAFF. *Doctor* CAIUS *comes one way, and steals away a fairy in green;* SLENDER *another way, and takes off a fairy in white; and* FENTON *comes, and steals away Mistress* ANNE PAGE. *A noise of hunting is heard; and all the Fairies run away.* FALSTAFF *rises up, pulls off his buck's head, and would escape, but* PAGE, FORD, *Mistress* PAGE, *and Mistress* FORD *confront him.*

Page. Nay, do not fly! I think we have watched
100 you now... [*Falstaff seeks to hide his face within the buck's head once again*
Will none but Herne the hunter serve your turn?

Mistress Page. I pray you, come, hold up the jest
no higher.... [*Falstaff casts the buck's head from him*
Now, good Sir John, how like you Windsor wives?
[*pointing to the horns*
See you these, husband? do not these fair yokes
Become the forest better than the town?

Ford. Now, sir, who's a cuckold now?—Master Brook, Falstaff's a knave, a cuckoldly knave—here are his horns, Master Brook...And, Master Brook, he hath enjoyed nothing of Ford's but his buck-basket, his cudgel, and
110 twenty pounds of money, which must be paid to Master Brook—his horses are arrested for it, Master Brook.

Mistress Ford. Sir John, we have had ill luck; we could never †mate...I will never take you for my love again, but I will always count you my deer.

Falstaff. I do begin to perceive that I am made an ass.

Ford. Ay, and an ox too: both the proofs are extant.

Falstaff. And these are not fairies! I was three or four times in the thought they were not fairies—and yet the guiltiness of my mind, the sudden surprise of my powers,
120 drove the grossness of the foppery into a received belief, in despite of the teeth of all rhyme and reason, that they were fairies....See now, how wit may be made a Jack-a-lent, when 'tis upon ill employment!

Evans [*returns, without his satyr-mask*]. Sir John Falstaff, serve Got, and leave your desires, and fairies will not pinse you.

Ford. Well said, fairy Hugh.

Evans. And leave you your jealousies too, I pray you.

Ford. I will never mistrust my wife again, till thou art able to woo her in good English. 130

Falstaff. Have I laid my brain in the sun, and dried it, that it wants matter to prevent so gross o'er-reaching as this? Am I ridden with a Welsh goat too? shall I have a coxcomb of frieze? 'tis time I were choked with a piece of toasted cheese.

Evans. Seese is not good to give putter; your pelly is all putter.

Falstaff. 'Seese' and 'putter'! Have I lived to stand at the taunt of one that makes fritters of English? This is enough to be the decay of lust and late-walking through 140 the realm.

Mistress Page. Why, Sir John, do you think, though we would have thrust virtue out of our hearts by the head and shoulders, and have given ourselves without scruple to hell, that ever the devil could have made you our delight?

Ford. What, a hodge-pudding? a bag of flax?

Mistress Page. A puffed man?

Page. Old, cold, withered, and of intolerable entrails?

Ford. And one that is as slanderous as Satan? 150

Page. And as poor as Job?

Ford. And as wicked as his wife?

Evans. And given to fornications, and to taverns, and sack, and wine, and metheglins, and to drinkings, and swearings and starings, pribbles and prabbles?

Falstaff. Well, I am your theme...you have the start of me, I am dejected...I am not able to answer the Welsh flannel. Ignorance itself is a plummet o'er me. Use me as you will.

Ford. Marry, sir, we'll bring you to Windsor, to one 160 Master Brook, that you have cozened of money, to whom you should have been a pandar: over and above that you have suffered, I think to repay that money will be a biting affliction.

Page. Yet be cheerful, knight: thou shalt eat a posset to-night at my house, where I will desire thee to laugh at my wife, that now laughs at thee...Tell her Master Slender hath married her daughter.

Mistress Page. Doctors doubt that...[*aside*] If Anne
170 Page be my daughter, she is, by this, Doctor Caius' wife.

SLENDER heard hulloing in the wood

Slender. Whoa, ho, ho! father Page!

Page. Son, how now! how now, son! have you dispatched?

Slender [*comes up*]. Dispatched! I'll make the best in Gloucestershire know on't; would I were hanged, la, else.

Page. Of what, son?

Slender. I came yonder at Eton to marry Mistress Anne Page, and she's a great lubberly boy....If it had not been i'th' church, I would have swinged him, or he should
180 have swinged me....If I did not think it had been Anne Page, would I might never stir—and 'tis a postmaster's boy!

Page. Upon my life, then, you took the wrong.

Slender. What need you tell me that? I think so, when I took a boy for a girl...If I had been married to him, for all he was in woman's apparel, I would not have had him.

Page. Why, this is your own folly. Did not I tell you, how you should know my daughter—by her garments?

190 *Slender.* I went to her in white, and cried 'mum,' and she cried 'budget,' as Anne and I had appointed, and yet it was not Anne, but a postmaster's boy.

Mistress Page. Good George, be not angry. I knew of

your purpose...turned my daughter into green--and, indeed, she is now with the doctor at the deanery, and there married.

CAIUS heard calling wrathfully

Caius. Vere is Mistress Page? [*comes up*] By gar, I am cozened! I ha' married un garçon, a boy; un paysan, by gar....a boy! It is not Anne Page—by gar, I am cozened!

Mistress Page. Why! did you take her in green? 200

Caius. Ay, by gar, and 'tis a boy: by gar, I'll raise all Windsor! [*he hurries away, shaking his fist*

Ford. This is strange...Who hath got the right Anne?

Page. My heart misgives me—here comes Master Fenton....

FENTON and ANNE PAGE appear, arm in arm

How now, Master Fenton!

Anne [*kneels*]. Pardon, good father! good my mother, pardon!

Page. Now, Mistress! how chance you went not with Master Slender?

Mistress Page. Why went you not with master doctor, maid? 210

Fenton. You do amaze her...Hear the truth of it.
You would have married her most shamefully,
Where there was no proportion held in love...
The truth is, she and I—long since contracted—
Are now so sure that nothing can dissolve us...
Th'offence is holy that she hath committed,
And this deceit loses the name of craft,
Of disobedience or unduteous title,
Since therein she doth evitate and shun
A thousand irreligious curséd hours, 220
Which forcéd marriage would have brought upon her.

Ford. Stand not amazed. Here is no remedy:
In love, the heavens themselves do guide the state—
Money buys lands, and wives are sold by fate.

Falstaff. I am glad, though you have ta'en a special stand to strike at me, that your arrow hath glanced.

Page. Well, what remedy? Fenton, heaven give
thee joy!
What cannot be eschewed, must be embraced.

Falstaff. When night-dogs run, all sorts of deer
are chased.

Mistress Page. Well, I will muse no further...
230 Master Fenton,
Heaven give you many, many merry days!
Good husband, let us every one go home,
And laugh this sport o'er by a country fire—
Sir John and all.

Ford. Let it be so. Sir John,
To Master Brook you yet shall hold your word,
For he to-night shall lie with Mistress Ford.

[*they troop homeward*

GLOSSARY

Note. Where a pun or quibble is intended, the meanings are distinguished as (*a*) and (*b*)

ACTÆON, transformed to a stag with horns and pursued by his own hounds—the classical prototype of the Elizabethan cuckold; 2. 1. 108; 3. 2. 39

ADDITIONS, titles; 2. 2. 275

AGAINST THE HAIR, i.e. against the grain—phrase derived from stroking an animal the wrong way; 2. 3. 36

AGGRAVATE HIS STYLE, i.e. give him a new title, raise him from 'knave' to 'cuckold'; 2. 2. 262

ALLHALLOWMAS, i.e. November 1st. Note that Simple is simple as regards the calendar; 1. 1. 190

ALLICHOLY, blunder for 'melancholy' (cf. *Two Gent.* 4. 2. 26); 1. 4. 148

AMAIMON, a mighty devil; cf. 1 *Hen. IV*, 2. 4. 370 and Scot, *Discoverie of Witchcraft* (ch. 29) 'king Baell or Amoimon'; 2. 2. 274

ANCHOR, 'the anchor is deep'; 1. 3. 50. If not corrupt, 'anchor' may have parallels in 'my invention...anchors on Isabel,' *Meas.* 2. 4. 3 and *Cym.* 5. 5. 393

ANTHROPOPHAGINIAN, man-eater; 4. 5. 8

ARMIGERO, i.e. 'armiger'=esquire possibly Slender uses the Italian form, more probably his Latinity is at fault; 1. 1. 8

AUTHENTIC, i.e. of established credit; 2. 2. 212

BAILLEZ, bring; 1. 4. 86

BANBURY CHEESE, a very thin cheese—referring to Slender's slenderness; Banbury was a notorious puritan centre and Bardolph may have this in mind also; 1. 1. 120

BARBASON, a prince of devils; cf. *Hen. V*, 2. 1. 57 and Scot, *Discoverie of Witchcraft*, xv. ii 'Marbas, alias Barbas, is a great president'; 2. 2. 274

BEAD, (*a*) a minute object; cf. *M.N.D.* 3. 2. 330; (*b*) prayer. N.B. It is Parson Hugh, albeit disguised, who gives him his holy commission; 5. 5. 49

BELL-WETHER, a ram with a bell at its neck to lead the flock. Ford led the 'rabble,' made much noise, and was a horned cuckold; 3. 5. 101

BETWEEN THIS AND HIS HEAD, a common phrase of the period in a similar connexion; 1. 4. 24

BILBO, a finely tempered sword, of Bilboa manufacture; 3. 5. 102

BOARD, (*a*) accost, address, (*b*) board a ship; 2. 1. 81–2

BOHEMIAN-TARTAR, v. *Hungarian*; 4. 5. 19

BOLD-BEATING, probably misprint for 'bowl-beating,' i.e. pot-thumping; 2. 2. 25

BOOK OF SONGS AND SONNETS, some miscellany of the period. Tottel's (1577) was entitled 'Songes and Sonnettes'; 1. 1. 184

BOY (to her), a hunting cry (v.

Turbervile, *Booke of Hunting*, p. 114); 1. 3. 53

BRAINFORD, i.e. Brentford; 4. 2. 70, etc.

BREAD AND CHEESE, usually taken as referring to the frugal fare in Falstaff's service, but N.E.D. gives it as a name of the cuckoo-bread flower, which is the point required here. Falstaff is the cuckoo in Page's nest (cf. 'cuckoo-birds,' 2. 1. 113), and his bread is cuckoo-bread; 2. 1. 123

BRIBED-BUCK, stolen deer; 5. 5. 24

BUCK, (*a*) male deer, stag; (*b*) dirty linen to be steeped in alkaline lye, as the first process in buck-washing or bleaching (cf. *whitsters*); 3. 3. 150, etc.

BUCKLERSBURY, a London street for grocers and apothecaries, whose shops were full of herbs 'in simple-time'; 3. 3. 69

BULLY, i.e. gallant (a term of endearment); 1. 3. 3, etc. For 'bully-stale' v. *stale*

BURN DAY-LIGHT, i.e. waste time; 2. 1. 48

BUTTONS, ''tis in his buttons,' probably a misprint for 'talons'; 3. 2. 63

CABBAGE, i.e. cabbage-head=fool; note the transition to 'broke your head'; 1. 1. 114

CANARY, (*a*) a lively Spanish dance; (*b*) sweet wine from the Canaries (cf. *pipe-wine*); 3. 2. 79

CANARIES, Quickly's confusion between *canary* (*a*) and 'quandary'; 2. 2. 58

CANE-COLOURED, possible 'weasel-coloured,' (v. N.E.D.), 1. 4. 21

CAREERS, 'passed the careers,' i.e. ran away with him (lit. 'galloped at full-speed over a race-course'); 1. 1. 166

CARRY, (i) 'carry-her,' probably Evans' pronunciation of 'career,' i.e. gallop; 1. 1. 222; (ii) 'carry't,' i.e. carry off the prize; 3. 2. 63

CARVE, make advances by signalling in a peculiar way with the fingers—'a sort of digitary ogle' (Lucas, *Webster* i. 209). Cf. *Err.* 2. 2. 121–2; *L.L.L.* 5. 2. 323 'A' can carve too and lisp' [1954], 1. 3. 44

CASHIER, (*a*) discard; (*b*) cheat, rob (? at cards); 1. 1. 165; 1. 3. 7

CASTILIAN-KING-URINAL, the urinal of Philip II of Spain; 2.3. 30

CATAIAN, i.e. inhabitant of Cathay. The Elizabethans had news of the wiles of 'the heathen Chinee' before Bret Harte; 2. 1. 130

CAT-A-MOUNTAIN, wild cat; 2. 2. 24

CHARACTERY, symbolical writing; 5. 5. 73

CHARINESS, scrupulous integrity; 2. 1. 90

CHEATER, (*a*) escheator, an official of the Exchequer; (*b*) sharper; 1. 3. 68

CHEESE, the Welshman's love of cheese was a popular subject of jest at this period; 1. 2. 11; 2. 2. 280; 5. 5. 82, 135

CLAPPER-CLAW, maul, thrash; 2. 3. 60

CLERKLY, (*a*) like a scholar; (*b*) smartly, artfully; 4. 5. 53

COG, cheat (at dice-play); 3. 1. 114; 3. 3. 44, 67

COME OFF, pay up; 4. 3. 11

CONY-CATCH, swindle—a cant term; the cony (=rabbit) was the dupe; 1. 1. 117; 1. 3. 33

Coram, i.e. quorum, a common corruption. Justices of Quorum, or Coram, were those who sat on the bench at county sessions; 1. 1. 5

Cornuto, horned cuckold (v. *peaking*); 3. 5. 66

Costard, head (lit. a large apple); 3. 1. 14

Cotsall, i.e. the Cotswolds, a favourite resort for coursing matches (spelt 'Cotsole', 2 *Hen. IV*, 3. 2. 24; 'Cotshall,' *Ric. II*, 2. 3. 9); 1. 1. 84

Council, (*a*) Privy Council, Star-chamber (q.v.); (*b*) ecclesiastical synod; 1. 1. 31–3

Counsel (in), in private; 1. 1. 112

Counter-Gate, (*a*) gate of debtor's prison, notorious for its smell (Falstaff had other reasons for his dislike); (*b*) ?=counter-gait, i.e. in the opposite direction; 3. 3. 75

Cowl-staff, a stout pole passed through the handles of a 'cowl' (lit. a water-tub), so that it could be hoisted by two men; 3. 3. 139

Coxcomb, fool's cap, in reference to Evans' satyr-head; 5. 5. 134

Cried-game, an insult the meaning of which is now lost (sporting slang); 2. 3. 81

Cry aim, applaud (archery term); 3. 2. 40

Curtal-dog, dog with docked tail, of no service in the chase; 2. 1. 100

Custalorum = contraction or corruption of 'custos rotulorum,' i.e. keeper of the rolls; 1. 1. 6

Cut and long-tail, i.e. horses or dogs of all sorts. Slender means 'Let them all come—under the degree of a squire,' i.e. so long as they are not too grand; 3. 4. 46

Datchet-mead, between Windsor Little Park and the Thames; 3. 3. 126, 141; 3. 5. 92

Daubery, false shows; 4. 2. 170

Deck (above), (*a*) above-board; (*b*) in reference to covering of any kind, clothes or sheets; 2. 1. 83

Devil-hern, devil-head (an allusion to Evans's horned mask); 5. 3. 11

Diffuséd, generally interpreted 'disorderly,' but possibly 'dispersed' (cf. 'burthen dispersedly,' *Temp.* 1. 2. 381); 1. 1. 55

Distance, v. *fencing*; 2. 1. 201; 2. 3. 23

Divinity, ? divination; 5. 1. 3

Draff, hog's wash; 4. 2. 100

Drumble, loiter, be sluggish; 3. 3. 139

Dutch dish, the German fondness for greasy cooking was evidently known in Shakespeare's day. Dutch = German; 3. 5. 109

Edward shovel-boards, old broad shillings of Edward VI, worn smooth by age and use, and therefore convenient for the game of Shovel-board or Shove-groat (cf. 2 *Hen. IV*, 2. 4. 207) in which the coin was flipped along a polished board into holes at the end of it; v. *Sh. Eng.* ii. 467–8. Slender paid 2*s.* 3*d.* apiece, no doubt on account of their excellent smoothness! 1. 1. 145

Egress and regress, a legal phrase, meaning right of entry, especially into harbours and waterways; the Host is quibbling on the name 'Brook'; 2. 1. 194

Eld, antiquity; 4. 4. 36

Entertain, engage in battle; 1. 3. 53: treat; 2. 1. 78

Ephesian, boon companion (cf. 2 *Hen. IV*, 2. 2. 164 'Ephesians of the old church'); 4. 5. 16

Equipage, usually taken to mean camp-follower's pickings or

stolen goods; but 'in equipage' =step by step (v. N.E.D. 'equipage' 14), and Pistol probably means 'in instalments'; 2. 2. 1

ERINGOES, candied roots of sea-holly, considered provocative; 5. 5. 20

ETHIOPIAN. The Host seems to have in mind 'Ethiops martial,' a metallic compound known to the old chemists and no doubt familiar to Dr Caius; 2. 3. 24

EVITATE, avoid; 5. 5. 219

EYAS-MUSKET, young male sparrow-hawk; 'the musket was 'the smallest and most insignificant [of the breed], yet a very smart little hawk...If taken from the nest, as an eyas, it would be also one of the tamest and most docile' (*Sh. Eng.* ii. 363)—all which is most applicable to Robin; 3. 3. 20

FALL=fault; 1. 1. 236

FALLOW, brownish-yellow; 1. 1. 83

FARTHINGALE (semi-circled), hooped skirt, extending behind but not in front of the body; 3. 3. 60

FAULT, (i) ''tis your fault.' This has puzzled many, but 'fault'='a check caused by failure of scent' and 'your' is used in a general sense (cf. 'your serpent in Egypt,' *Ant.* 2. 7. 29). The comment is quite in Shallow's usual manner (cf. ''tis the heart,' 2. 1. 202); 1. 1. 87. (ii) ''Tis my fault,' i.e. 'it is my misfortune'; 3. 3. 208

FEE'D, employed (lit. 'hired' like a servant, v. N.E.D.); 2. 2. 184

FEE-SIMPLE, WITH FINE AND RECOVERY (in), i.e. in absolute possession, under the strongest legal sanction (cf. *Sh. Eng.* i. 405–6). Mrs Page is perhaps thinking of the 'twenty pounds' (=fine) and the attempt to bring Falstaff to his senses in Act 5 (=recovery); 4. 2. 205–6

FELLOW OF THIS WALK, i.e. the keeper or forester of this beat, to whom would be due a shoulder after a kill. Windsor Forest was divided up into 'walks.' Falstaff quibbles, meaning that he will keep his shoulders to fight the keeper, should he appear; 5. 5. 25

FENCING (cf. 1. 1. 265–70; 2. 1. 198–204; 2. 3. 13–24), an innovation in Shakespeare's day. Justice Shallow, of the old school, sighs for the days of the long sword, which the new-fangled rapier has ousted. Dr Caius, as Frenchman, represents the new school (v. *Sh. Eng.* ii. 389–407). TERMS: *distance* = the regulation interval to be kept between the fencers; *foin*, *veney*, *stoccado* (or *stock*) and *punto* = different kinds of hits or thrusts; *reverse* = punto reverso or back-handed thrust; *montant* = the montanto or upright blow

FICO, Italian for 'fig'; 1. 3. 29

FIGHTS, canvas screens to conceal men on ship-board, before going into action; 2. 2. 128

FIGURE, (i) 'by the figure' = ?by astrological figures or by making waxen figures for the purpose of enchantment; 4. 2. 170. (ii) 'Scrape the figures' etc., i.e. clear your husband's brain of phantasms; 4. 2. 210

FIND YOU, unmask you: Evans seems to think he means to strip her; 4. 2. 135

FIXTURE, poise, tread; 3. 3. 58

FLANNEL, 'the Welsh flannel,' in

reference to Evans' disguise; flannel and frieze (q.v.) were of Welsh manufacture at this period; 5. 5. 158

FLAX, possibly misprint for 'flux', i.e. a discharge of blood or other matter from the body; 5. 5. 147

FOIN, v. *fencing*; 2. 3. 21

FOPPERY, dupery, deceit; 5. 5. 120

FRAMPOLD, crusty, disagreeable; 2. 2. 86

FRANCISCO, Frenchman, with a quibble perhaps on 'francisc' = battle-axe; 2. 3. 25

FRETTED, worked, fermented (v. N.E.D. 'fret' vb. 10, which does not quote this passage). Cf. 'distillation'; Falstaff means that the clothes had enough grease of their own without his, to make them ferment; 3. 5. 104

FRIEZE, a coarse cloth with a nap, v. *flannel*; 5. 5. 134

FROTH AND LIME, 'to froth' = to give short measure by frothing the ale overmuch; 'to lime' = to mitigate the sourness of wine or ale by doctoring it with lime; 1. 3. 15

GALLIMAUFRY, medley, i.e. promiscuity; 2. 1. 105

GEMINY, pair; 2. 2. 9

GING, old form of 'gang'; 4. 2. 113

GOLIATH WITH A WEAVER'S BEAM, cf. 2 *Sam.* xxi. 19 'the staff of Goliath's spear was like a weaver's beam'; 5. 1. 20

GOOD AND FAIR (a technical expression), cf. Turbervile, *Booke of Hunting*, ch. 6 'the tokens whereby a man may knowe a good and fayre hound'; 1. 1. 91

GOOD EVEN AND TWENTY, i.e. good day and plenty of them! ('even' = any time after noon); 2. 1. 177

GOOD-JER (or 'good-year'), unexplained; N.E.D. describes it as 'a meaningless expletive,' but 'the good-years shall devour them flesh and fell' (*Lear* 5. 3. 24) implies something definite and evil; 1. 4. 119

GOT'S LORDS AND HIS LADIES, possibly Evans' expansion of the expletive 'God's lud' = God's Lord; 1. 1. 221

GOTTEN IN DRINK. Cowards were credited with this origin; 1. 3. 22

GOT-'UDGE ME, i.e. God judge me; 1. 1. 172

GOURD AND FULLAM, species of false dice; 1. 3. 84

GRATED, worried, pestered; 2. 2. 6

GREAT CHAMBER, large reception-room. These were a new feature in houses of this period and only found in those of the wealthy; Slender is bragging as usual (v. *Sh. Eng.* ii. 60); 1. 1. 144

GREEN-SLEEVES (the tune of), an amorous ballad-tune, associated somehow with harlotry: *Stat. Reg.* (Sept. 15, 1580) enters 'Greene Sleves moralised to the Scripture, declaringe the manifold benefites and blessinges of God bestowed on sinfull menne'; 2. 1. 57; 5. 5. 19

GROAT, 'seven groats in mill-sixpences'; a groat = fourpenny piece; mill-sixpences = newly introduced machine-made coins, with hard edges, to replace the older crudely hammered coins. 'Slender's words are *pour rire* in two senses, (*a*) the impossibility of reckoning the sum that way, (*b*) the confusion between the old groat (a time-honoured unit of value with immemorial traditions) and the latest mechanical improvement in coinage' (Prof. George Unwin: privately); but v. *British Numismatic Journ.* 3rd Ser. III, 291; 1. 1. 145

HACK, 'these knights will hack.' 'Hack' appears to mean 'to take to the road as a highwayman,' or (of a female) 'to become a harlot' (cf. 'hackney,' *L.L.L.* 3. 1. 35). N.E.D. gives 'hack' (vb.[3] 3*b*)='to ride on the road; as distinguished from cross-country or military riding,' but quotes only 19th cent. instances. Hart shows good reason for thinking the jest refers to the 'Cales (i.e. Cadiz) Knights' created by the Earl of Essex in 1596. Note the possibility of word-play in 'Alice' and 'Cales' or 'Calice'; this is the only occasion on which we learn Mrs Ford's Christian name; 2. 1. 46

HAPPY MAN BE HIS DOLE, proverbial=may his dole (i.e. lot) be that of a happy man; 3. 4. 65

HAVE WITH YOU, i.e. 'Let's go together'; 2. 1. 141, 197; 3. 2. 83

HAVING, property; 3. 2. 65

HAVIOUR, appearance; 1. 3. 77

HAWK FOR THE BUSH, a short-winged hawk for quarry such as pheasants, rabbits, etc. in woodland country (v. *Sh. Eng.* ii. 363–4); 3. 3. 221

HEART OF ELDER, i.e. of pith, as contrasted with 'heart of oak'; 2. 3. 26

HEROD OF JEWRY, a type of outrageous audacity (cf. *Ant.* 3. 3. 3); 2. 1. 17

HICK AND HACK, copulate. Cf. Nashe, *Choice of Valentines*, l. 114, and 'hackney' in G. of *L.L.L.*; 4. 1. 59

HIGH AND LOW, false dice, so loaded as to cast high or low numbers at will; 1. 3. 85

HODGE-PUDDING, a large sausage of boar's or hog's meat, still a dainty in the West of England; 5. 5. 147

HOLE MADE IN YOUR BEST COAT, proverbial=flaw in your reputation; 3. 5. 129

HONESTY, honour; 2. 1. 91, etc.

HORN-MAD, mad with rage like a bull; 1. 4. 47; (with a quibble on the cuckold's horn), 3. 5. 138

HOT=hit; 1. 1. 268

HOT BACKS, hot-backed=lustful; 5. 5. 11

HUNGARIAN, in reference to discarded and cashiered soldiers from Hungary (cf. 'base Phrygian Turk' 1. 3. 87, 'Bohemian-Tartar' 4. 5. 19). In 1593 war broke out between the Empire and the Turks and lasted until 1606; 1. 3. 20

ILL, (*a*) savage, (*b*) miserable, which is the meaning Mrs Ford takes up (v. N.E.D.); 2. 1. 31

INSTALMENT, seat in which a Knight of the Garter was installed; 5. 5. 63

INTOLERABLE, excessive; 5. 5. 149

JACK, knave; 1. 4. 55, 114

JACK-A-LENT, dressed-up puppet for boys to throw at in Lent; 3. 3. 24; 5. 5. 122

JACK-AN-APES, lit. 'monkey,' but Evans means a satyr, which was a kind of 'ape'; 4. 4. 68

JAYS, symbolical of loose women; 3. 3. 39

KIBES, chilblains; 1. 3. 32

Kissing-comfits, perfumed sugar-plums, used by women to sweeten their breath; 5. 5. 20

Knot, band, company; 3. 2. 46; 4. 2. 113

Labras, Pistol's blunder for 'labra,' lips; 1. 1. 152

Laroon, thief (v. note); 1. 4. 67

Latten, tin; 1. 1. 151

Legend of angels, i.e. legion of angels, but with a quibble on the Golden Legend; 1. 3. 52

Life is a shuttle. Cf. *Job* vii. 6 'My days are swifter than a weaver's shuttle,' 5. 1. 21

Liquor, grease, oil (vb.); 4. 5. 90

Luce, (*a*) pike (fresh-water), (*b*) hake, cod (salt-water); 1. 1. 14, 19

Lunes, (*a*) fits of lunacy, (*b*) leashes for hawks, (*c*) astrological figures; 4. 2. 20

Lurch, pilfer; 2. 2. 23

Marry trap. N.E.D. does not explain, but Dr Johnson interprets 'an exclamation of insult, when a man was caught in his own stratagem' (cf. *Ham.* 3. 2. 247); 1. 1. 156

Mechanical salt-butter rogue, 'mechanical' = base, 'salt-butter' = (*a*) perhaps a contemptuous reference to Ford's station in life as a trader, (*b*) lecherous cuckold, 'butter' referring to the horn; 2. 2. 257

Melt me out of my fat. 'Fat' here has the secondary meaning of 'slow wit,' cf. 1. *Hen. IV*, 1. 2. 2 'fat-witted'; 4. 5. 89

Mephostophilus; 1. 1. 122. Pistol maybe thinking of Marlowe's *Dr Faustus*, 1. 3. 32–3:

How pliant is this Mephostophilis:
Full of obedience and humility.

Metheglins, a Welsh variety of mead; 5. 5. 154

Middle earth (man of), i.e. mortal (v. N.E.D. 'middle-erd'); 5. 5. 80

Mill-sixpences, v. *groat*; 1. 1. 145

Mince, i.e. trip it. Cf. *Isaiah* iii. 16 '...the daughters of Sion are haughty and walk with stretched forth necks and wanton eyes, walking and mincing as they go': the 1611 version explains 'mincing' as 'tripping nicely'; 5. 1. 8

Mocked, (*a*) deceived, (*b*) ridiculed; 5. 3. 17–18

Mock-water, 'muck-water' (liquid manure), possibly with a quibble on 'make water'; 2. 3. 52

Montant, v. *fencing*; 2. 3. 24

Mountain-foreigner, cf. 'mountain-squire' (*Hen. V*, 5. 1. 37); 1. 1. 150

Mumbudget. Cotgrave gives 'to play at Mumbudget, or be at a Non-plus,' and Nashe (McKerrow, iii. 124) uses it as the cry of one who is baffled; probable derived from some children's game. Surely Anne Page suggested this 'nay-word.' Note that Slender gets the 'budget'—of the post-boy. 5. 2. 6; 5. 5. 190

Mummy, a pulpy substance or mass (N.E.D.); 3. 5. 17

Mussel-shell, i.e. empty fool, perhaps with a quibble upon 'muzzle'; 4. 5. 26

Nay-word, pass-word, watch-word; 2. 2. 118; 5. 2. 5

No-verbs, usually interpreted 'words which do not exist,' but possibly = nay-words (q.v.); 3. 1. 99

Nurse, housekeeper; 1. 2. 3; 3. 2. 58

Nuthook, i.e. catchpole, constable. 'Nutcrackers' was likewise a cant term for a pillory. N.B. the quibble in 'the very note of it'; 1. 1. 156

Nym, to nim = to steal, filch

Obsequious, zealous, dutiful; 4. 2. 2

Od's nouns, perversion of 'God's wounds'; 4. 1. 22

Oeillades, sheep's eyes, amorous glances; 1. 3. 59

O'er-looked, i.e. with the evil eye; 5. 5. 83 [4. 2. 192

Open, give tongue (like a hound);

Ouph, elf; lit. 'elf's child, changeling'; 4. 4. 50; 5. 5. 57

Ox, 'to make an ox of one' = to make one a fool; here with special reference to the horns (cf. *Troil.* 5. 1. 66); 5. 5. 116 [5. 5. 41

Oyes, i.e. 'oyez', the crier's call;

Pack, plot, conspiracy; 4. 2. 113

Passant, (*a*) excellently, (*b*) heraldic term, 'of a beast, walking and looking towards the dexter side with one forepaw raised' (N.E.D.); 1. 1. 17

Peaking cornuto, i.e. 'slinking (or prying) cuckold,' with a quibble upon 'peak,' i.e. the point of the horn; 3. 5. 66

Peck, a round vessel used as a peck measure; 3. 5. 102

Pensioners, i.e. 'the gentlemen pensioners' or royal body-guard. Quickly ranks them above earls on account of their splendid uniform (cf. *M.N.D.* 2. 1. 10);

Period, goal; 3. 3. 42 [2. 2. 73

Perpend, ponder; 2. 1. 105

Pheazar, i.e. Vizier (Hart); 1. 3. 10

Phlegmatic, blunder for 'choleric'; Quickly attempts the talk of physicians; 1. 4. 74

Phrygian Turk, v. *Hungarian*; 1. 3. 87

Pickt-hatch, 'your manor of Pickthatch,' a disreputable quarter of London. Hart quotes Randolph, *Miser's Looking-glass*, 'my Pickthatch graunge and Shoreditch farm'; 2. 2. 17

Pink, (*a*) a fishing-vessel (v. N.E.D.), (*b*) a fashionable beauty; 2. 2. 127

Pinnace, (*a*) a light vessel, often in attendance upon a larger one, (*b*) go-between, bawd. Hart quotes Heywood, *Edward IV*, pt i, 'Farewell, pink and pinnace, flibote and carvel'; 1. 3. 79

Pipe-wine, wine from the wood (with quibbles on pipe = musical instrument and 'whine'); 3. 2. 80

Pittie-ward, possibly 'petty-ward', possibly 'Pity-ward' (with a connexion with the Church of the Blessed Virgin in Windsor); 3. 1. 5

Plummet, (*a*) a woollen fabric (N.E.D. 'plumbet')—quibble on 'flannel' (q.v.), (*b*) plummet-line, for fathoming; 5. 5. 158

Potatoes, i.e. the 'batata' or sweet potato, considered provocative; 5. 5. 19 [28

Pottle = 2 quarts; 2. 1. 191; 3. 5.

Prat, prats = buttocks (N.E.D.). Ford is as good as his quibble; 4. 2. 178

Precisian, puritan; 2. 1. 5

Predominate, an astrological term, carrying on the 'meteor' simile; 2. 2. 260

Preeches, Evans means 'breeched,' i.e. whipped; 4. 1. 70

Preparations, accomplishments (N.E.D. gives no other instance of this meaning); 2. 2. 213

Primero, a popular card-game (v. *Sh. Eng.* ii. 473); 4. 5. 93

Puddings, sausages, entrails stuffed with meat (cf. *hodge-pudding* and 1 *Hen. IV*, 2. 4. 498); 2. 1. 27
Pumpion, pumpkin; 3. 3. 38
Punto, v. *fencing*; 2. 3. 23

Quality, profession, business (cf. *Temp.* 1. 2. 193); 5. 5. 40
Quean, hussy; 4. 2. 166
Quittance, discharge from debt, receipt; 1. 1. 9

Rag, worthless creature (N.E.D.); 4. 2. 179
Ragg'd, jagged; 4. 4. 31
Ratolorum, Slender of course means 'rotulorum' (v. *Custalorum*) and it seems possible that Shakespeare intended him to say so, the reading of the text being a scribal error. The use of the correct form would be sufficiently egregious here in itself, since it shows that Slender is unconscious that he is virtually repeating Shallow's 'Custalorum'; 1. 1. 7
Rattles, i.e. bladders with dried peas or beans inside; 4. 4. 52
Ravens (young), (*a*) cf. *Psal.* cxlvii. 9, (*b*) birds or beasts of prey (N.E.D. 'ravin' 2 *b*, *c*), i.e. sharks; 1. 3. 35
Red-lattice, i.e. of the ale-house—red-lattice windows being commonly found in ale-houses; 2. 2. 25
Register, catalogue; 2. 2. 175
Respect, reputation; 3. 1. 55
Reverse, v. *fencing*; 2. 3. 23
Ringwood, popular Elizabethan name for a hound (v. Golding's *Ovid*, iii, 270); 2. 1. 108
Ronyon, 'of obscure origin' (N.E.D.), perhaps connected with 'roinish,' 'ronyous' = scabby (cf. *Macb.* 1. 3. 6); 4. 2. 180

Sack, general name for white Spanish or Canary wines; 2. 1. 8, etc.; 'burnt sack,' i.e. hot drink made of sack and sugar; 2. 1. 192, etc.
Sackerson, a famous bear at Paris garden in Shakespeare's day; 1. 1. 278
Sadness, seriousness; 4. 2. 85
Salt butter, v. *mechanical salt butter*; 2. 2. 257
Sauce them, i.e. make it hot for them; 4. 3. 11
Scall, i.e. 'scald,' scabby; 3. 1. 113
Scut, (*a*) the short tail of a hare or deer, (*b*) N.E.D. quotes 15th cent. example = 'skirt,' which may also be intended here; 5. 5. 18
Sea-coal, i.e. coal brought by sea from Newcastle, as distinguished from charcoal; 1. 4. 8
Season, 'of the season,' i.e. in the rutting-season; 3. 3. 152
Seese, Welsh pronunciation of 'cheese' (q.v.); 1. 2. 11; 5. 5. 136
Sentences, 'out of his five sentences.' Possibly a blunder for 'senses' as Evans supposes; but cf. Lyly, *Euphues* (Bond ii. 158), 'Hungry stomackes are not to be fed with sayings against surfettings, nor thirst to be quenched with sentences against drunkennesse,' which suggests that Slender had a Book of Moral Maxims in his library; 1. 1. 163
Shaft or bolt on't (make a), proverbial = do one thing or another. A shaft was an arrow for the long-bow, a bolt a shorter one for the cross-bow; if the wood was too short for the one it would do for the other (*Sh. Eng.* ii. 381); 3. 4. 24

SHELVY, made of shelves or sand-banks; 3. 5. 14

SHENT, rated, scolded; 1. 4. 34

SHIP-TIRE, head-dress shaped like a ship, or having a ship-like ornament; 3. 3. 53

SHORT KNIFE AND A THRONG, i.e. the cut-purse's requisites; 2. 2. 16

SHOVEL-BOARDS, v. *Edward shovel-boards*; 1. 1. 145

SHOWER SING IN THE WIND (cf. *Temp.* 2. 2. 20). Possibly connected with the noise of missiles or arrows (note 'shoot point blank,' l. 31); 3. 2. 34

SIDES, i.e. thighs, loins; 5. 5. 25

SIMPLES, herbs. Dr Caius finds a Simple in his closet; 1. 4. 62

SIT AT, i.e. live at; 1. 3. 9

SLICE, generally taken as referring to the 'Banbury cheese'; but the three sharpers are challenging Slender to utter the 'matter in his head,' and 'slice' may therefore be the hawking term for 'mute'; cf. 'pass good humours' (1. 1. 155) and Wither, *Brit. Rememb.* (1628), 'Our Herneshaws, slicing backward, filth on those Whose worths they dare not openly oppose,' which seems very apt to the present situation; 1. 1. 124

SLIGHTED, possibly for 'sleighted' (conveyed dexterously) with a quibble on 'slided'; 3. 5. 9

SOFTLY-SPRIGHTED, a polite way of saying he was a coward; 1. 4. 22

SPRAG, mispronunciation of 'sprack' = brisk, alert; 4. 1. 74

STALE, (*a*) dupe, laughing-stock (v. N.E.D. 'stale' sb.[3] 6), (*b*) urine of cattle, with a quibble upon 'bully' (i.e. bull), cf. 'Castilian-King-Urinal'; 2. 3. 26

STAND (a special), i.e. a sheltered position or covert for shooting at game (cf. *L.L.L.* 4. 1. 7–10; 3 *Hen. VI*, 3. 1. 1–4; *Sh. Eng.* ii. 386); 5. 5. 226

STAND, waste time with; 3. 3. 119

STAR-CHAMBER MATTER, the King's Council, sitting in the Star-chamber, exercised jurisdiction in regard to 'such offences as riots, slanders and libels, or even criticisms of magistrates.' In 1590 a deer-stealing case was before it (*Sh. Eng.* i. 384–5, ii. 162); 1. 1. 2

STARINGS, 'swearings and starings.' McKerrow (*Nashe*, iv. 100) writes: 'The two words are very frequently thus used in conjunction. To "stare" seems...to mean little more than to swagger, to behave in an overbearing and offensive manner'; 5. 5. 155; cf. 'stare,' 2. 2. 258

STEWED PRUNES, a common term for prostitutes from the 'stews'; 1. 1. 267

STILL SWINE EATS ALL THE DRAFF, proverb = 'the quiet sow eats all the hog's-wash or refuse'; 4. 2. 100

STOCCADOES, v. *fencing*; 2. 1. 201

STOCK = *stoccado*; 2. 3. 23

STONES, testicles; 1. 4. 109

STOPPED, stuffed; 3. 5. 103

STRAIN, disposition; 2. 1. 80; 3. 3. 176

SUBMISSION, confession; 4. 4. 11

SUCH ANOTHER NAN, cf. *Troil.* 1. 2. 282, 'You are such another woman,' where the meaning seems to be 'a very woman'; 1. 4. 145

SUFFERANCE, distress; 4. 2. 2

SURGE, i.e. of sweat; 3. 5. 111

SWINGE, (*a*) beat, (*b*) have sexual intercourse (v. N.E.D. 'swinge' vb. 1 *e*); 5. 5. 179–80

TAKE, bewitch; 4. 4. 32

TALLOW, 'piss my tallow.' Cf. Turbervile, *Booke of Hunting* (1576), p. 45: 'During the time of their [i.e. the harts'] rut...their chief meat is the red mushroom or Todestoole which helpeth well to make them pysse their greace'; 5. 5. 14

TESTER, sixpence; 1. 3. 86

THRUMMED HAT, i.e. made of weaver's thrums, or possibly fringed with them so as to conceal the wearer's face; 4. 2. 72

TIGHTLY, safely, i.e. like a 'tight ship' (cf. *Temp.* 5. 1. 225); 1. 3. 78: soundly; 2. 3. 60

TINDERBOX, a hit at Bardolph's 'fiery exhalations'; 1. 3. 25

TIRE-VALIANT, some kind of fanciful head-dress; 3. 3. 53

TRIAL-FIRE, Hart quotes Fletcher, *Faithful Shepherdess*, 5. 2:

In this flame his finger thrust,
Which will burn him if he lust;
But if not away will turn
As loth unspotted flesh to burn;

5. 5. 84

TROW, wonder; 1. 4. 128; 2. 1. 57

TRUCKLE-BED, small couch on castors; 4. 5. 6

TURTLES, i.e. turtle-doves, proverbial for fidelity; 2. 1. 72; 3. 3. 39

UNTAPIS, come out of cover or hiding, see O.E.D.; 3. 3. 157

UNKENNEL, unearth; kennel=fox's hole (cf. *Ham.* 3. 2. 86); 3. 3. 156

UNRAKED, i.e. not banked up with ashes to keep the fire in all night; 5. 5. 44

URCHINS, hedgehogs, or devils in that form; 4. 4. 50

VAGRAM (cf. 'vagrom' *Ado*, 3. 3. 26), Evans gets confused between 'fragrant' (l. 19) and 'vagrant'; 3. 1. 24

VENEY, v. *fencing*; 1. 1. 267

VIZAMENTS, advisements. Evans means 'consider that seriously'; 1. 1. 35

VLOUTING-STOG, i.e. flouting-stock = laughing-stock; 3. 1. 111; 4. 5. 74

WARRENER, rabbit-keeper, not a very fearsome antagonist, rabbits being gentle beasts; 1. 4. 25

WATCHED, i.e. caught in the act (cf. 2 *H. VI*, 1. 4. 45); 5. 5. 100

WEATHERCOCK, referring to the page's fantastic attire; a weathercock often had a pennon attached to it (cf. *L.L.L.* 4. 1. 96, 'What plume of feathers is he that indited this letter? What vane? What weathercock?'); 3. 2. 16

WHITING, bleaching; 3. 3. 125

WHITSTERS, bleachers; 3. 3. 13

WINK, close the eyes; 5. 5. 48

WITTOL, a contented cuckold; 2. 2. 274

YEA AND NO (by), a puritan expletive; 1. 1. 81; 1. 4. 92; 4. 2. 187

YELLOWS, i.e. jaundice, generally of horses, but being a disease of the liver, formerly supposed the seat of the passions, also used for jealousy in man; 1. 3. 98

YOKE, couple; 2. 1. 157

YOKES, horns (perhaps with a quibble on 'oaks'=oak-boughs); 5. 5. 104

YOUTH IN A BASKET, proverbial= fortunate lover (Hart); 4. 2. 112

WORDSWORTH CLASSICS

General Editors: Marcus Clapham & Clive Reynard

JANE AUSTEN
Emma
Mansfield Park
Northanger Abbey
Persuasion
Pride and Prejudice
Sense and Sensibility

ARNOLD BENNETT
Anna of the Five Towns

R. D. BLACKMORE
Lorna Doone

ANNE BRONTË
Agnes Grey
The Tenant of Wildfell Hall

CHARLOTTE BRONTË
Jane Eyre
The Professor
Shirley
Villette

EMILY BRONTË
Wuthering Heights

JOHN BUCHAN
Greenmantle
Mr Standfast
The Thirty-Nine Steps

SAMUEL BUTLER
The Way of All Flesh

LEWIS CARROLL
Alice in Wonderland

CERVANTES
Don Quixote

G. K. CHESTERTON
Father Brown: Selected Stories
The Man who was Thursday

ERSKINE CHILDERS
The Riddle of the Sands

JOHN CLELAND
Memoirs of a Woman of Pleasure: Fanny Hill

WILKIE COLLINS
The Moonstone
The Woman in White

JOSEPH CONRAD
Heart of Darkness
Lord Jim
The Secret Agent

J. FENIMORE COOPER
The Last of the Mohicans

STEPHEN CRANE
The Red Badge of Courage

THOMAS DE QUINCEY
Confessions of an English Opium Eater

DANIEL DEFOE
Moll Flanders
Robinson Crusoe

CHARLES DICKENS
Bleak House
David Copperfield
Great Expectations
Hard Times
Little Dorrit
Martin Chuzzlewit
Oliver Twist
Pickwick Papers
A Tale of Two Cities

BENJAMIN DISRAELI
Sybil

THEODOR DOSTOEVSKY
Crime and Punishment

SIR ARTHUR CONAN DOYLE
The Adventures of Sherlock Holmes
The Case-Book of Sherlock Holmes
The Lost World & Other Stories
The Return of Sherlock Holmes
Sir Nigel

GEORGE DU MAURIER
Trilby

ALEXANDRE DUMAS
The Three Musketeers

MARIA EDGEWORTH
Castle Rackrent

GEORGE ELIOT
The Mill on the Floss
Middlemarch
Silas Marner

HENRY FIELDING
Tom Jones

F. SCOTT FITZGERALD
A Diamond as Big as the Ritz & Other Stories
The Great Gatsby
Tender is the Night

GUSTAVE FLAUBERT
Madame Bovary

JOHN GALSWORTHY
In Chancery
The Man of Property
To Let

ELIZABETH GASKELL
Cranford
North and South

KENNETH GRAHAME
The Wind in the Willows

GEORGE & WEEDON GROSSMITH
Diary of a Nobody

RIDER HAGGARD
She

THOMAS HARDY
Far from the Madding Crowd
The Mayor of Casterbridge
The Return of the Native
Tess of the d'Urbervilles
The Trumpet Major
Under the Greenwood Tree

NATHANIEL HAWTHORNE
The Scarlet Letter

O. HENRY
Selected Stories

HOMER
The Iliad
The Odyssey

E. W. HORNUNG
Raffles: The Amateur Cracksman

VICTOR HUGO
The Hunchback of Notre Dame
Les Misérables: volume 1
Les Misérables: volume 2

HENRY JAMES
The Ambassadors
Daisy Miller & Other Stories
The Golden Bowl
The Turn of the Screw & The Aspern Papers

M. R. JAMES
Ghost Stories

JEROME K. JEROME
Three Men in a Boat

JAMES JOYCE
Dubliners
A Portrait of the Artist as a Young Man

RUDYARD KIPLING
Captains Courageous
Kim
The Man who would be King & Other Stories
Plain Tales from the Hills

D. H. LAWRENCE
The Rainbow
Sons and Lovers
Women in Love

SHERIDAN LE FANU
(edited by M. R. James)
Madam Crowl's Ghost & Other Stories

JACK LONDON
Call of the Wild & White Fang

HERMAN MELVILLE
Moby Dick
Typee

H. H. MUNRO
The Complete Stories of Saki

EDGAR ALLAN POE
Tales of Mystery and Imagination

FREDERICK ROLFE
Hadrian the Seventh

SIR WALTER SCOTT
Ivanhoe

WILLIAM SHAKESPEARE
All's Well that Ends Well
Antony and Cleopatra
As You Like It
A Comedy of Errors
Hamlet
Henry IV Part 1
Henry IV part 2
Henry V
Julius Caesar
King Lear
Macbeth
Measure for Measure
The Merchant of Venice
A Midsummer Night's Dream
Othello
Richard II
Richard III
Romeo and Juliet
The Taming of the Shrew
The Tempest
Troilus and Cressida
Twelfth Night
A Winter's Tale

MARY SHELLEY
Frankenstein

ROBERT LOUIS STEVENSON
Dr Jekyll and Mr Hyde

BRAM STOKER
Dracula

JONATHAN SWIFT
Gulliver's Travels

W. M. THACKERAY
Vanity Fair

TOLSTOY
War and Peace

ANTHONY TROLLOPE
Barchester Towers
Dr Thorne
Framley Parsonage
The Last Chronicle of Barset
The Small House at Allington
The Warden

MARK TWAIN
Tom Sawyer & Huckleberry Finn

JULES VERNE
Around the World in 80 Days & Five Weeks in a Balloon
20,000 Leagues Under the Sea

VOLTAIRE
Candide

EDITH WHARTON
The Age of Innocence

OSCAR WILDE
Lord Arthur Savile's Crime & Other Stories
The Picture of Dorian Gray

VIRGINIA WOOLF
Orlando
To the Lighthouse

P. C. WREN
Beau Geste

Distribution

AUSTRALIA, BRUNEI
& MALAYSIA
Reed Editions
22 Salmon Street, Port Melbourne
Vic 3207, Australia
Tel: (03) 245 7111
Fax (03) 245 7333

CZECH REPUBLIC
Bohemian Ventures spol s r o
Delnicka 13
170 00 Prague 7
Tel: 02 877837 Fax: 02 801498

DENMARK
BOG-FAN
St. Kongensgade 65
DK-1264 København K

FRANCE
Chiron Diffusion
40, rue de Seine, Paris 75006
Tel: 1 43.26.47 56 Fax: 1 45.83.54.63

GERMANY, AUSTRIA
& SWITZERLAND
Swan Buch-Marketing GmbH
Goldscheuerstrabe 16
D-7640 Kehl Am Rhein, Germany

GREAT BRITAIN & IRELAND
Wordsworth Editions Ltd
Cumberland House, Crib Street,
Ware, Hertfordshire SG12 9ET

Selecta Books
The Selectabook
Distribution Centre
Folly Road, Roundway, Devizes
Wiltshire SN10 2HR

SCOTLAND
Lomond Books
36 West Shore Road, Granton,
Edinburgh EH5 1QD

INDIA
OM Book Service
1690 First Floor
Nai Sarak, Delhi – 110006
Tel: 3279823-3265303 Fax: 3278091

IRAN
World Book Distributors
No 26 Behrooz Street, Suit 6
Tehran 19119
Tel: 9821 8714622 Fax: 9871 50044

ISRAEL
Timmy Marketing Limited
Israel Ben Zeev 12
Ramot Gimmel, Jerusalem
Tel: 02-865266 Fax: 02-880035

ITALY
Magis Books SRL
Via Raffaello 31/C
Zona Ind Mancasale, 42100 Reggio Emilia
Tel: 0522-920999 Fax: 0522-920666

PHILIPPINES
I J Sagun Enterprises
P O Box 4322 CPO Manila
2 Topaz Road, Greenheights Village
Taytay, Rizal Tel: 631-80-61 TO 66

PORTUGAL
International Publishing Services Ltd
Rua da Cruz da Carreira, 4B,1100 Lisboa
Tel: 01-570051 Fax: 01-3522066

SINGAPORE
Book Station
18 Leo Drive, Singapore
Tel: 4511998 Fax: 4529188

SLOVAK REPUBLIC
Slovak Ventures spol s r o
Stefanikova 128, 94901 Nitra
Tel/Fax: 087 25105

CYPRUS
Huckleberry Trading
4 Isabella, Anavargos, Pafos, Cyprus
Tel: 06-231313

SOUTH AFRICA
Struik Book Distributors (Pty) Ltd
Graph Avenue, Montague Gardens,
7441 P O Box 193 Maitland 7405
South Africa
Tel: (021) 551-5900 Fax: (021) 551-1124

SPAIN
Ribera Libros, S.L.
Poligono Martiartu, Calle 1 – nº 6
48480 Arrigorriaga, Vizcaya
Tel: 34-4-6713607 (Almacen)
34-4-4418787 (Libreria)
Fax: 34-4-6713608 (Almacen)
34-4-4418029 (Libreria)

USA, CANADA & MEXICO
Universal Sales & Marketing
230 Fifth Avenue, Suite 1212
New York, N Y 10001 USA
Tel: 212-481-3500 Fax: 212-481-3534

DIRECT MAIL
Redvers
Redvers House, 13 Fairmile,
Henley-on-Thames, Oxfordshire RG9 2JR
Tel: 0491 572656 Fax: 0491 573590